AF594797

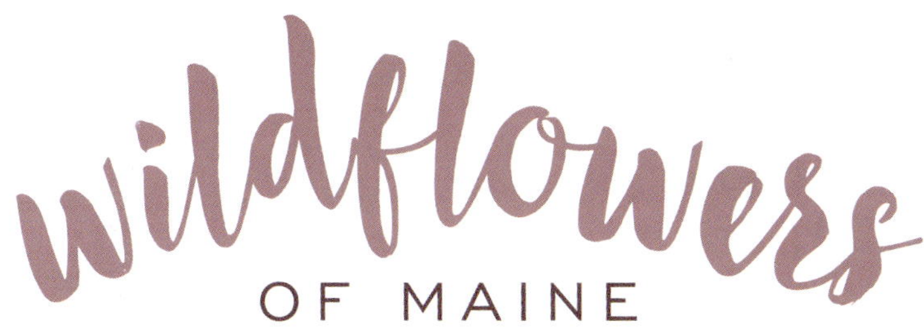
wildflowers
OF MAINE

Down East Books

Published by Down East Books
An imprint of The Globe Pequot Publishing Group, Inc.
64 South Main Street
Essex, CT 06426
www.globepequot.com

Distributed by NATIONAL BOOK NETWORK

Cover and interior design by Piper Wallis and Chloe Batch

British Library Cataloguing in Publication Information available

Library of Congress Cataloging-in-Publication Data available

ISBN 978-1-60893-655-7 (hardcover)
ISBN 978-1-60893-656-4 (e-book)

Printed in India

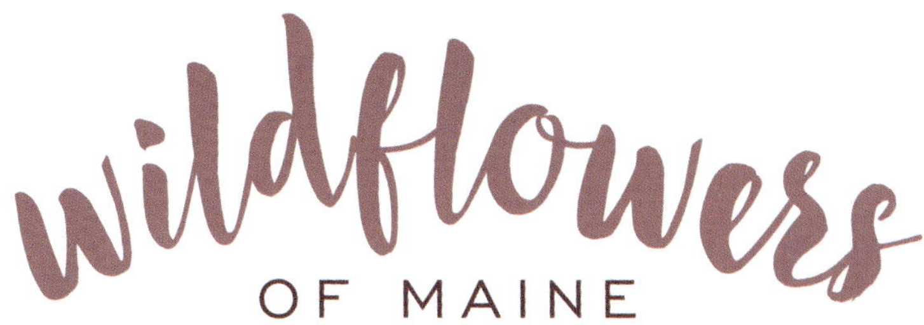

OF MAINE

BOTANICAL ART OF

KATE FURBISH

WITH BIOGRAPHICAL ESSAY BY

MELISSA DOW CULLINA

Down East Books

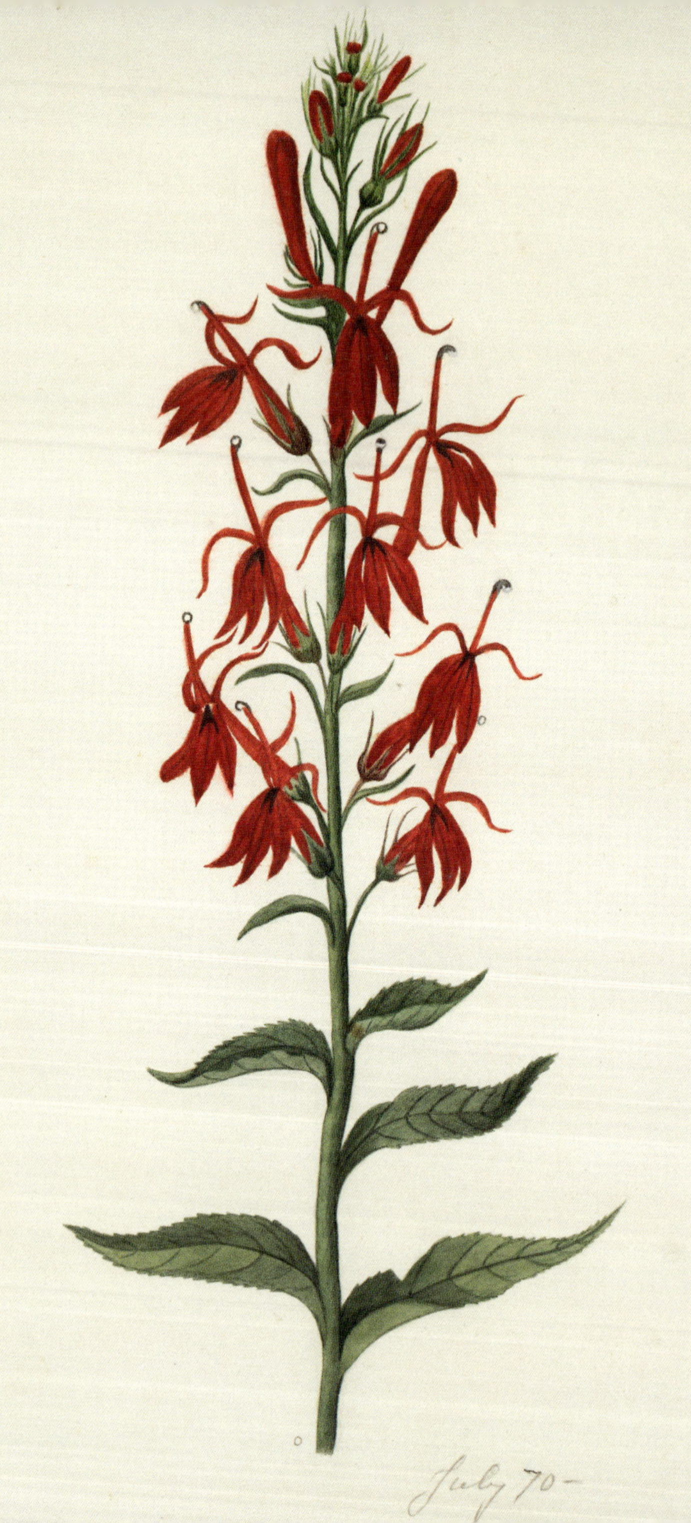
July 70-

"I do not claim artistic merit but merely a truthful
representation of what I saw in the plants,
free from all decorative effects."

–kate furbish

letter to William De Witt Hyde,
Bowdoin College President, December 22, 1908

IN THE EARNEST PURSUIT OF HER CALLING

Kate Furbish and the Wildflowers of Maine

Over nearly a century, Catherine "Kate" Furbish (1834–1931) lived a remarkably full and productive life in the earnest pursuit of her calling: botany. She sought to observe and collect the vast diversity of plants from across the state of Maine—exploring its bogs, forests, fields, mountains, and shores—to fulfill her great goal of completing a collection of scientifically accurate portraits of the flora of Maine. On her life's journey, she befriended many who shared her keen interest in plants, including other well-remembered botanists of her time. She helped found the Josselyn Botanical Society of Maine and was herself a highly-

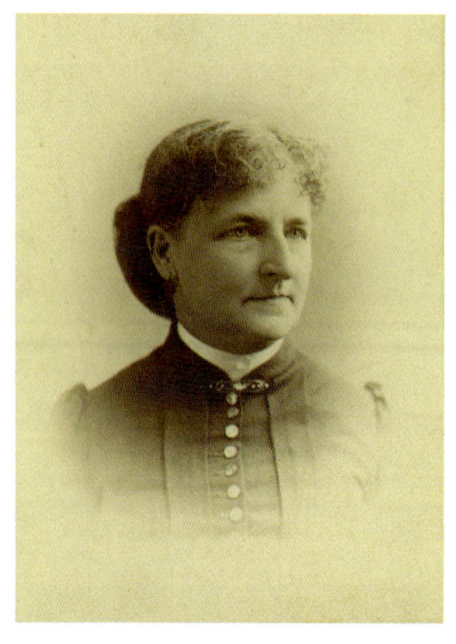

regarded member of the botanical community. Through more than thirteen hundred detailed illustrations, as well as the specimens that made those renderings possible, she left behind a body of work that has ensured her stature in the minds of New England botanists today. In natural history circles, her ambition, work, and tenacity of purpose is nothing short of legendary.

Born in Exeter, New Hampshire, Kate was the first child and only daughter of Benjamin and Mary Lane Furbish. A year after her birth, the family relocated to the prosperous town of Brunswick, Maine, which Kate would call home for the rest of her life. In Brunswick, five younger brothers were born, three of whom survived infancy. Benjamin Furbish was a merchant with a thriving hardware store. He began teaching young Kate at the age of twelve to identify the local wildflowers and plants.

Kate attended a private school for girls, where it is likely she was exposed to botany, a popular area of study for young ladies at the time. And, like many of her contemporaries, Kate also studied Latin, which undoubtedly contributed to her ease with botanical nomenclature and her understanding of the descriptive meanings of many Latin scientific names. She also trained in drawing and art from an early age, taking lessons in both Portland and Boston.

Furbish emerged as a young botanist at age twenty-one, when in the spring of 1856 she made a series of plant collections from the woods and grounds around Brunswick. In April, she discovered and collected a spring harbinger, mayflower, "in woods." And in May, around the time of her twenty-second birthday, she collected several more spring wildflowers, including trout lily "in rich open grounds, bulb deep in the ground," and the delicate dwarf ginseng "in low woods." She also collected and pressed spring-blooming trees that month; the emerging coppery leaves and white blossoms of the smooth shadbush attracted her attention, as did the spikes of mountain maple flowers. She identified and collected a few more plants that season, mostly from the wild, but one butterfly weed came from a garden. This set of early Furbish specimens, housed at the University of Maine Herbaria, provides a unique glimpse into her early botanical explorations and reveals that she was enchanted by "botanizing" even in her early twenties. She was in good company.

". . . nineteenth century American attitudes towards women's education resulted in many young women having sound background to study plants independently . . . . with the result that professional botanists had a wide audience who understood their activities and supported them." —E.D. Rudolph

---

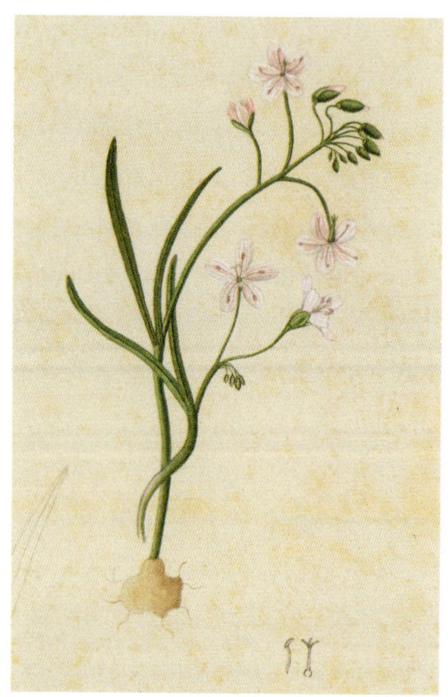

Carolina spring beauty
(Claytonia caroliniana)

One such professional was Professor Asa Gray, then a professor of natural history at Harvard University. In 1858, shortly after Furbish's first collecting forays, Gray published *How Plants Grow: A Simple Introduction to Structural Botany with a Popular Flora.* Furbish used and recommended this book, which popularized "Botany for Young People" by explaining and illustrating plant growth, the types of leaves and fruits, and how plants are classified. The second portion of the book was a "popular flora," which contained the "common wild plants of the country." Furbish wrote of this volume later in life: "I am very fond of Gray's 'How Plants Grow.' I have never outgrown it."

A lapse in botanical collecting during her mid-20s to early 30s might be attributed in part to the onset of the Civil War. In the fall of 1861 Kate's father was elected to the Maine Congress and she accompanied him to Augusta for part of the legislative session. Like many young women, she visited hospitalized soldiers and helped make bandages for the wounded. She wrote to her cousin: "how your heart would ache, dear Millie, if you should go into a hall where there were 134 men stretched on beds of suffering, and away from their homes."

Furbish greatly enjoyed visiting extended family and travelling, often making long visits to relatives in Boston and Wells. On one of her stays in Boston she attended a series of botany lectures for teachers that re-kindled her interest in botany. Meanwhile during roughly the same period, in 1867, Furbish was studying painting while spending the winter with family in Boston. She wrote to cousin Millie, "I am taking two lessons a week all the time and practice the best part of every day." Her interests in botany and art were converging in a meaningful way, and in these years just prior to her first great outpouring of work, she was formulating her ambitious plan to create a full collection of Maine botanical illustrations, which she would title "Maine Flora."

Regrettably it was also then, and intermittently throughout her life, that she was plagued with neuralgia, a nerve disorder that caused pain in her hands and feet. She frequently mentions periods of illness in her correspondence to friends and family, but her determination to remain productive through the pain and challenges of her condition is evident in the sheer volume of work she created.

I have catalogued 103 plants in four days which have peeped out of the ground far enough to be named.

Little is known about the true beginnings of Furbish's great artistic-scientific project. In the labels that she prepared to accompany her drawings, however, Furbish herself provides a clue to its inception. Only

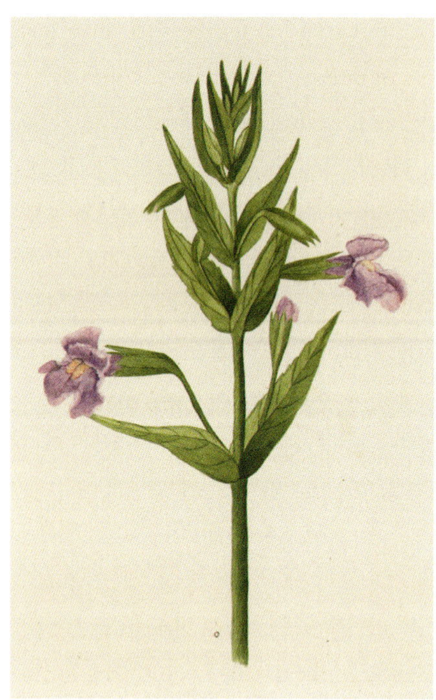

Allegheny monkey flower
(Mimulus ringens)

two paintings among her extensive collection, those for water lobelia and Indian pipe, have observation dates as early as 1869—giving them the distinction of likely being the earliest paintings in her collection.

It is widely acknowledged that Kate Furbish began her life's work in earnest in 1870, when she resumed botanizing with vigor and enthusiasm in familiar haunts. That first year she collected and mounted numerous charismatic wildflowers of Brunswick, including columbine, monkey flower, gaywings, windflower, pitcher plant, and early saxifrage. She explored habitats close to home in Brunswick, Topsham, and Harpswell. An impressive 107 of her illustrations cite associated plants found during that active period. Most of these labels also cite later observations of these plants in other parts of Maine, and it is nearly certain that not all 107 paintings were completed that year.

Furbish's detailed and precisely rendered illustrations were created in stages, often after studying multiple specimens over several years. First, she sketched the plant in the life stage in which she first saw or collected it, later adding flowers or fruit if those features were absent from her first collection. She then painted her graphite sketch with watercolors to achieve a rendering that she considered true to life.

Throughout the early 1870s Furbish actively sought and collected plants while continuing work on her drawing and paintings. Both of her parents were becoming feeble by then and must have required her steady care; perhaps explaining why she observed and recorded fewer plants in these years than in the remarkably productive year of 1870.

Her concern was primarily with the faithful and scientifically accurate representation of her subject, not a necessarily pleasing image; so her work should be considered most closely aligned with scientific illustration rather than fine art. Yet it is difficult not to think of her work in the same way we consider the work of Audubon, another naturalist whose paintings have transcended science.

Showing the pluck and exploratory spirit she would become known for, Kate Furbish in the early 1870s collected specimens from many environs typical to coastal Maine: bearberry from open, rocky places; seaside buttercup and herbaceous sea-blite from the shore; little floating heart and water smartweed from lakes and ponds; and skunk cabbage and white turtlehead from the swamps.

Her life as intrepid field botanist was underway.

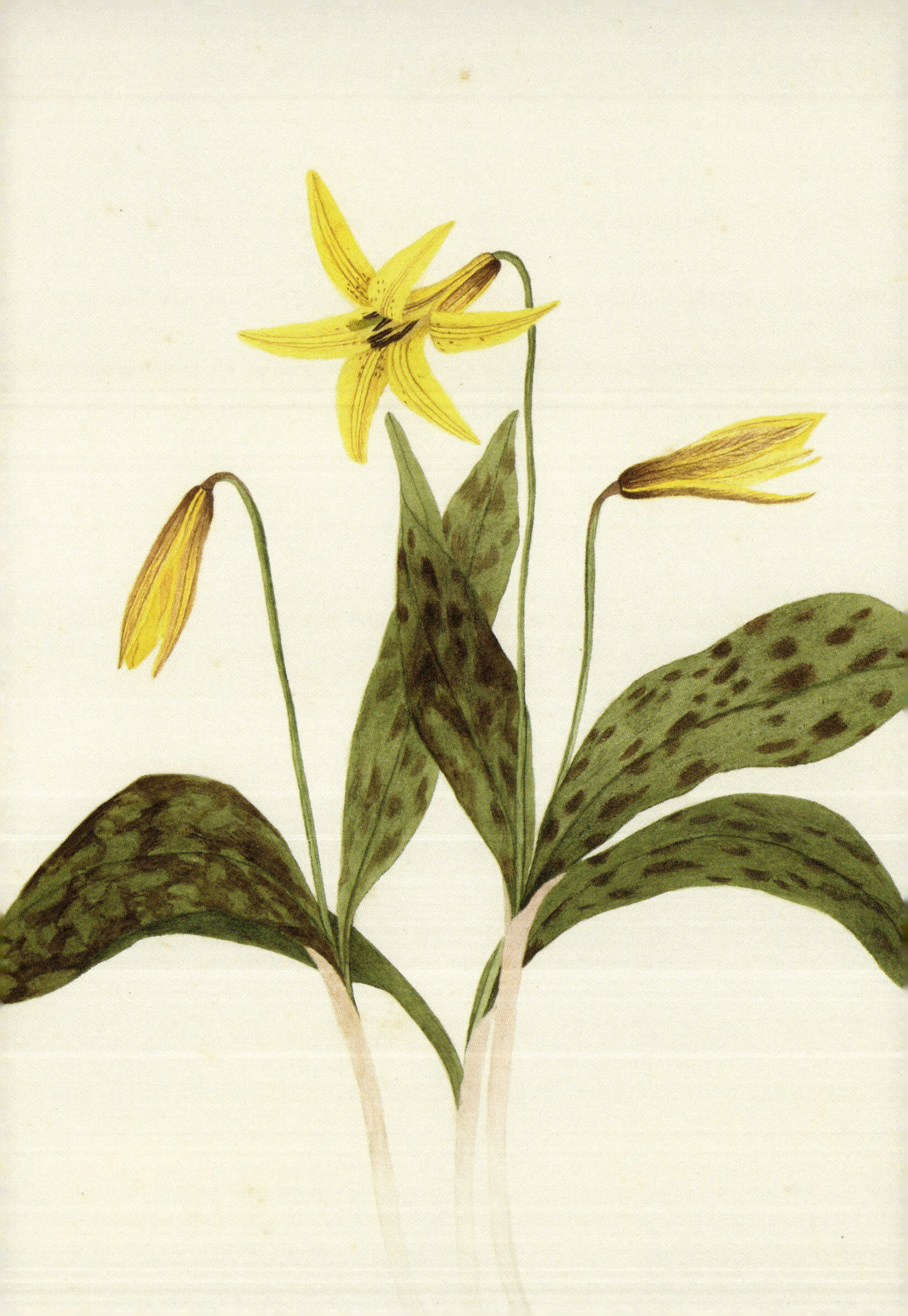

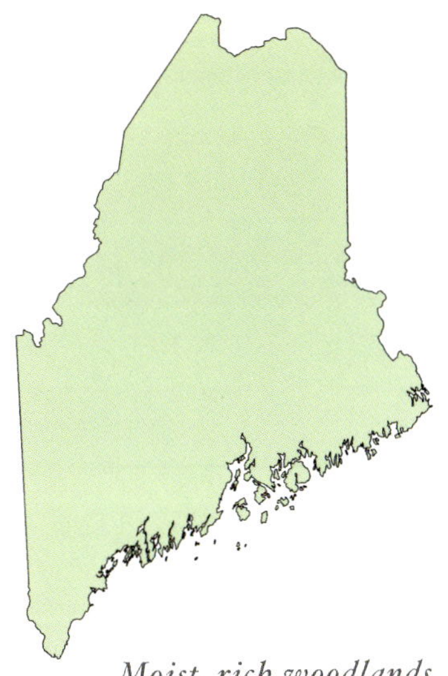

Moist, rich woodlands

Furbish Observed At:

Location unknown

AMERICAN TROUT LILY

Erythronium americanum

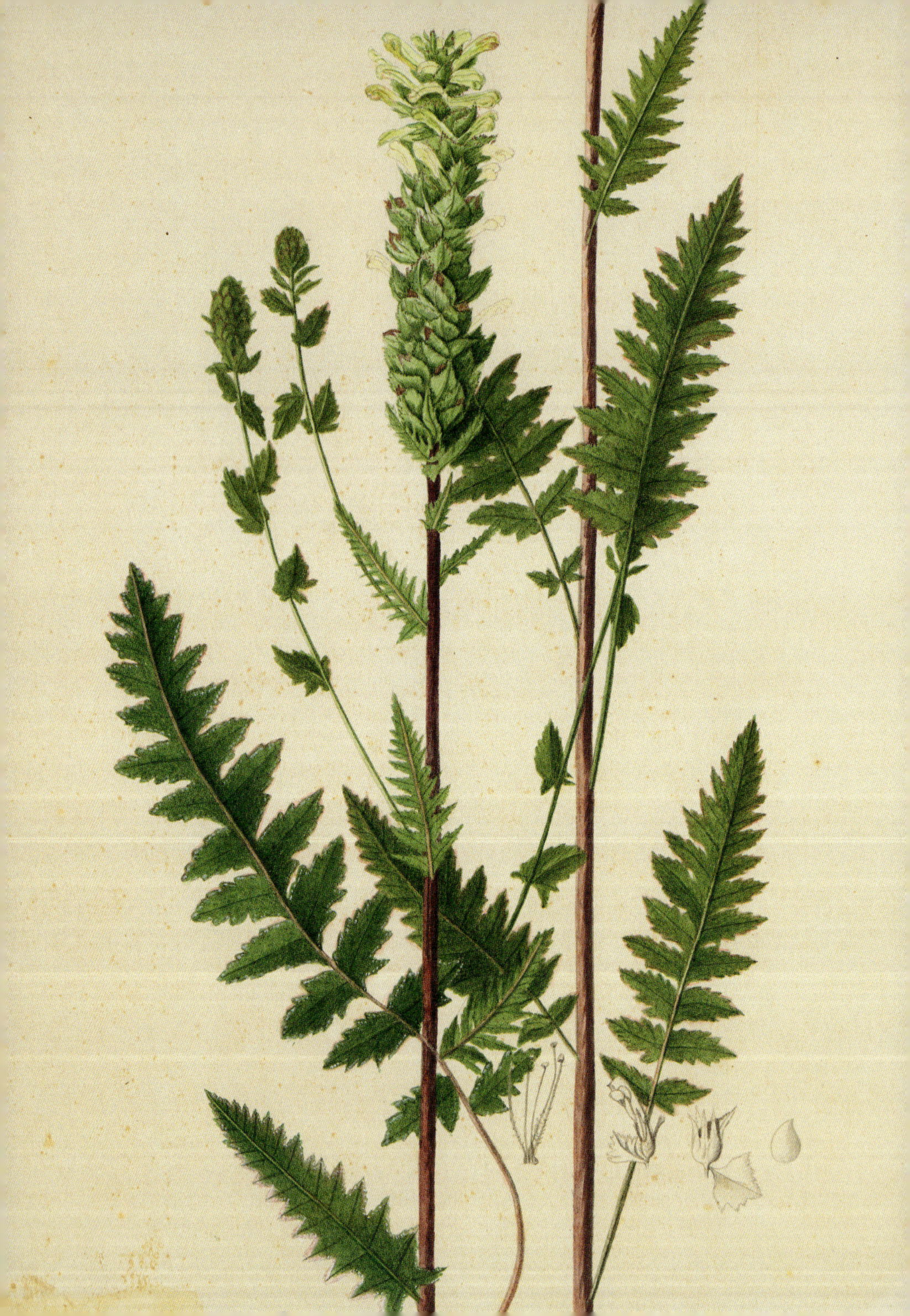

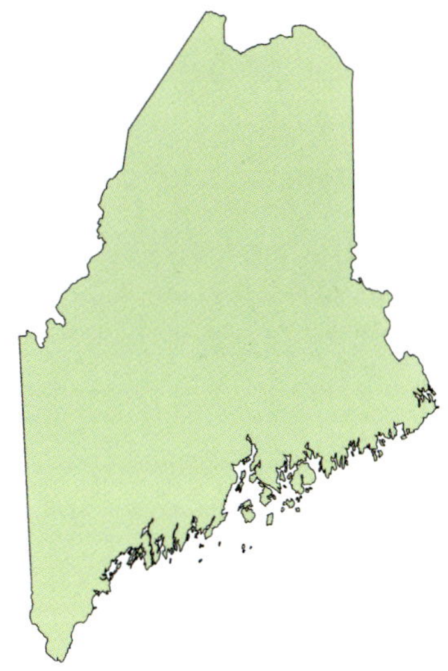

Banks of the St. John River

Furbish Observed At:

Location withheld to protect endangered species

FURBISH'S LOUSEWORT

Pedicularis furbishiae

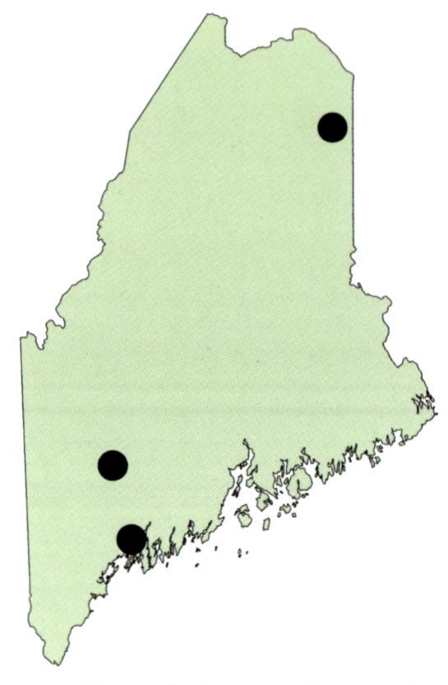

Open ledges, rocky banks, cliffs, and dry meadows

Furbish Observed At:

Brunswick (1870)
Fort Fairfield (1880)
East Livermore (n.d.)

SCOTCH BELLFLOWER

Campanula rotundifolia

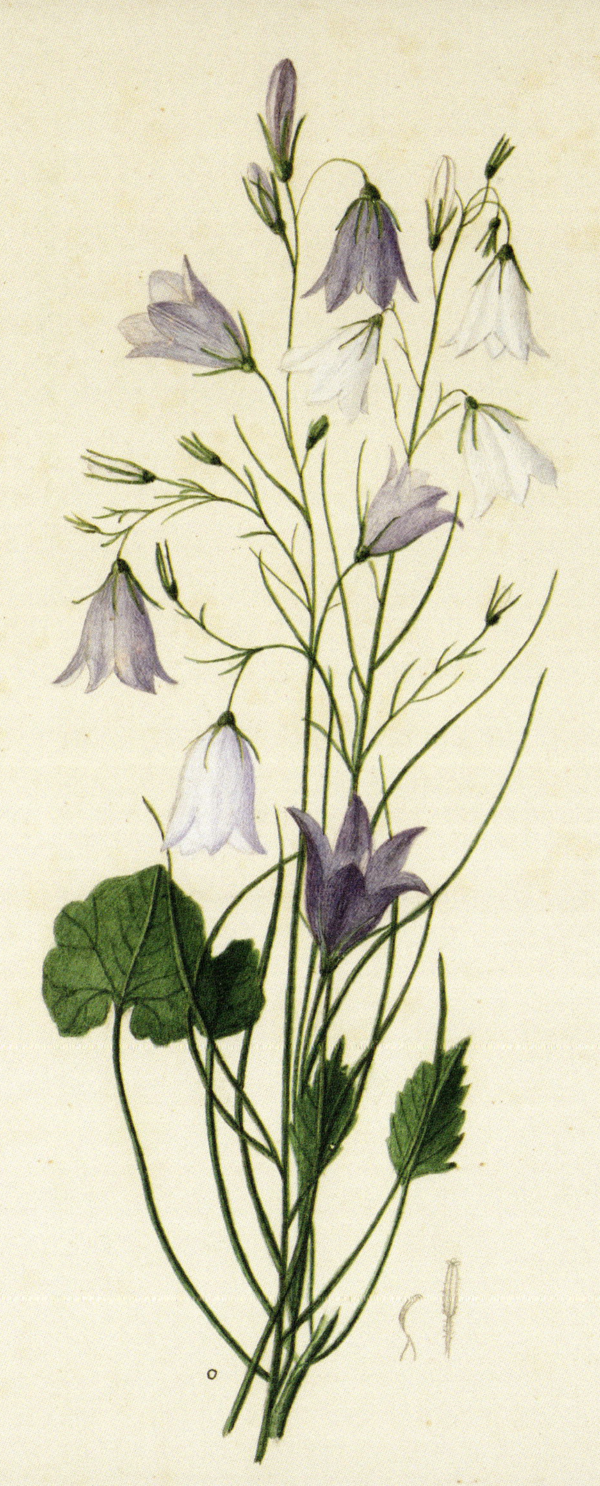

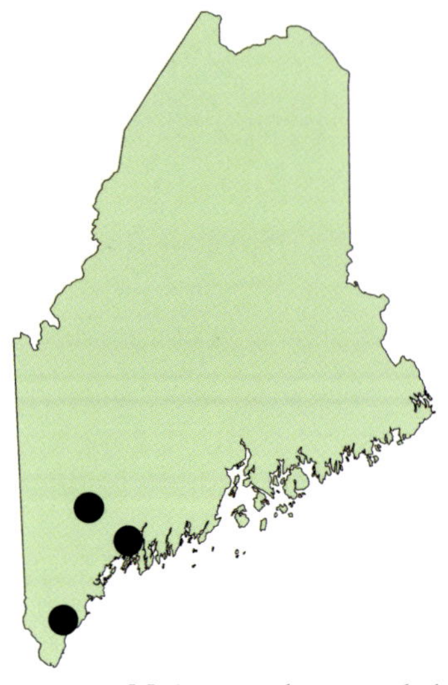

Moist meadows and thickets

Furbish Observed At:

Brunswick (1896)
South Poland (1896)
Wells (1898)

Note: Andrew's bottle gentian does not actually occur in Maine. It is possible Furbish thought she was drawing Andrew's bottle gentian, when in fact it was *Gentiana clausa* (closed bottle gentian).

ANDREW'S BOTTLE GENTIAN

Gentiana andrewsii

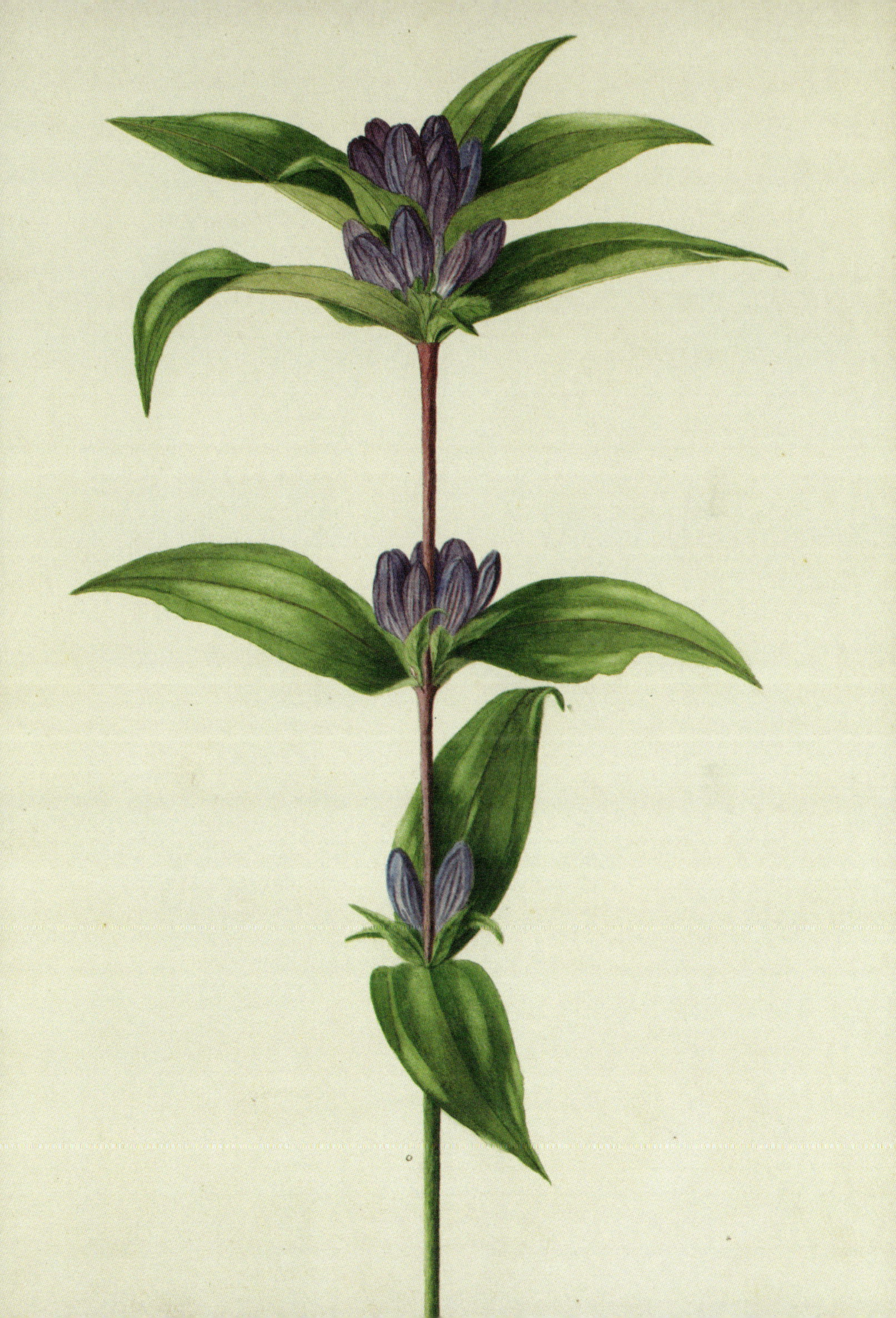

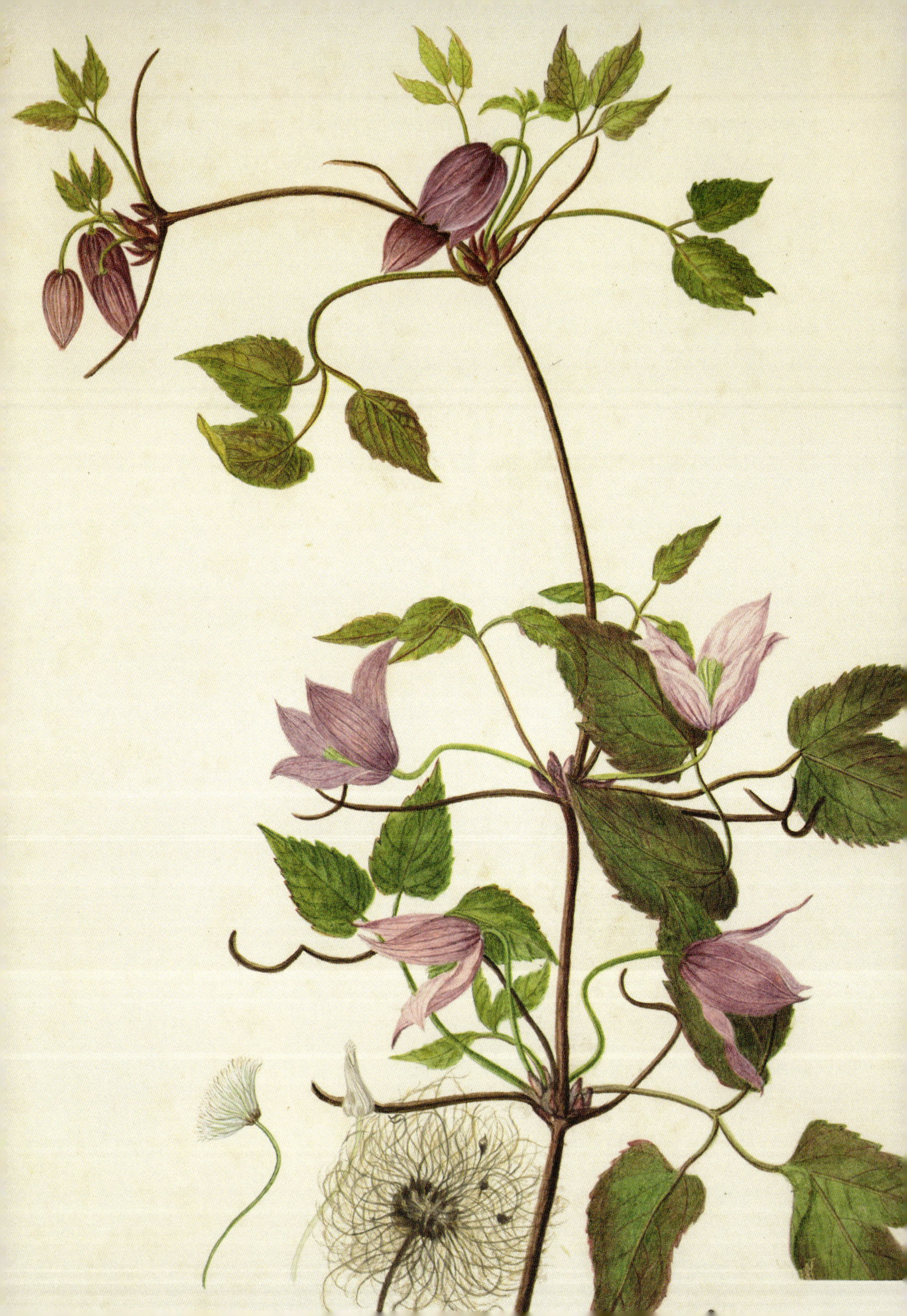

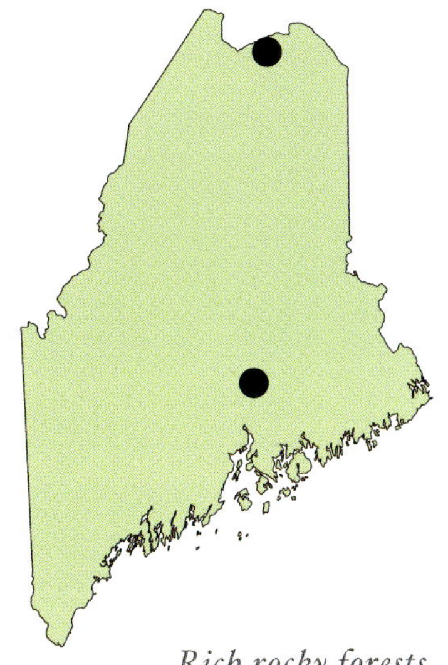

Rich rocky forests,
ridges, and ledges

Furbish Observed At:

Orono (1881)
Fort Kent (1881)

PURPLE VIRGIN'S BOWER

Clematis occidentalis

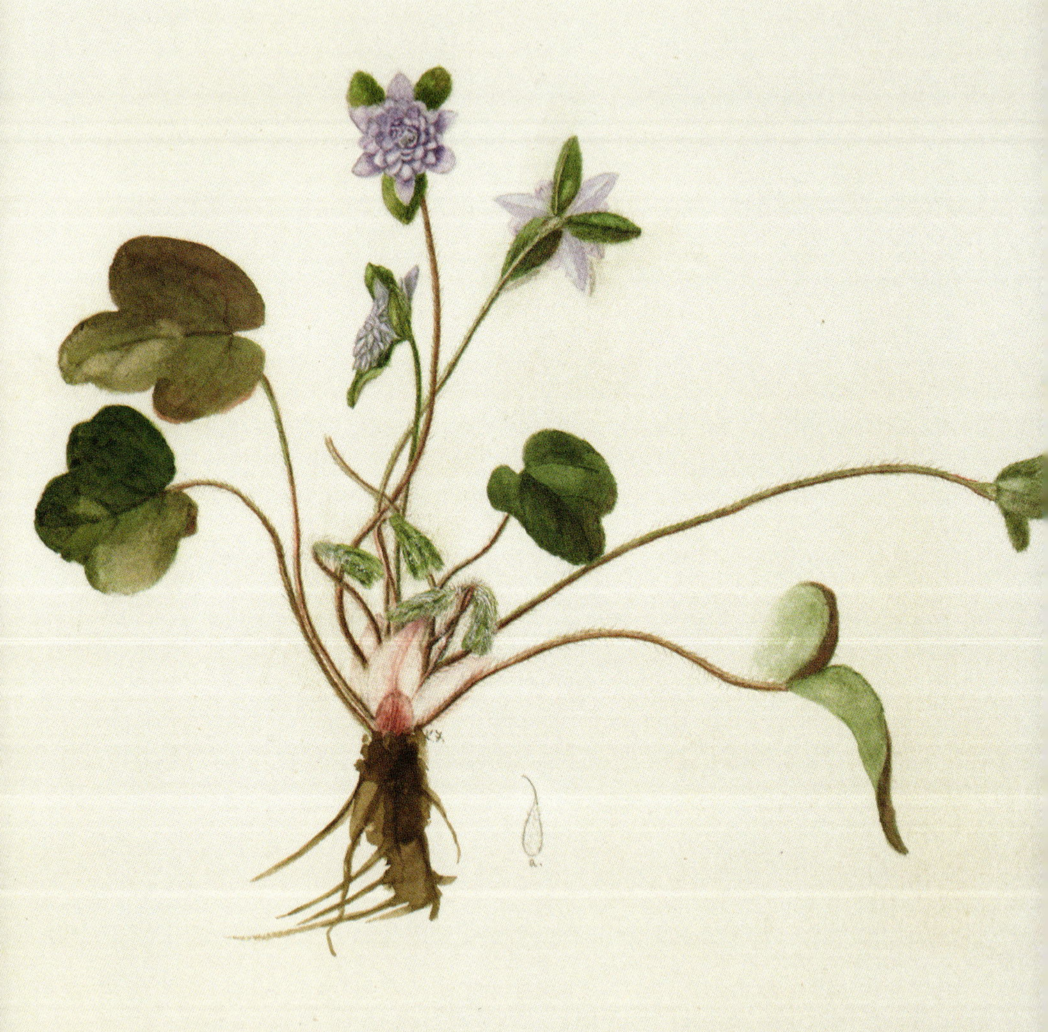

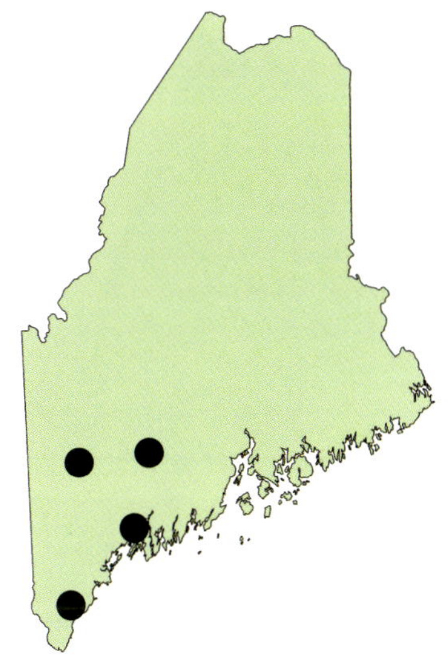

Dry forests

Furbish Observed At:

Fayette (1878)
Brunswick (1890)
Wells (1898)
Snow's Falls (1905)

BLUNT LOBED HEPATICA

Anemone americana

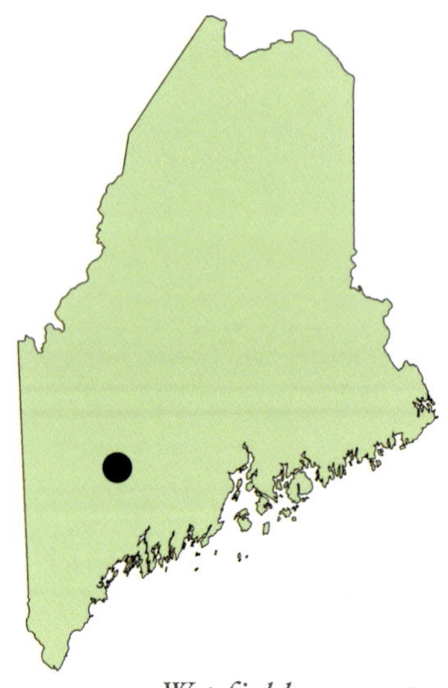

Wet fields, swamps,
and stream sides

Furbish Observed At:

Livermore Falls (1875)

TALL MEADOW RUE

Thalictrum pubescens

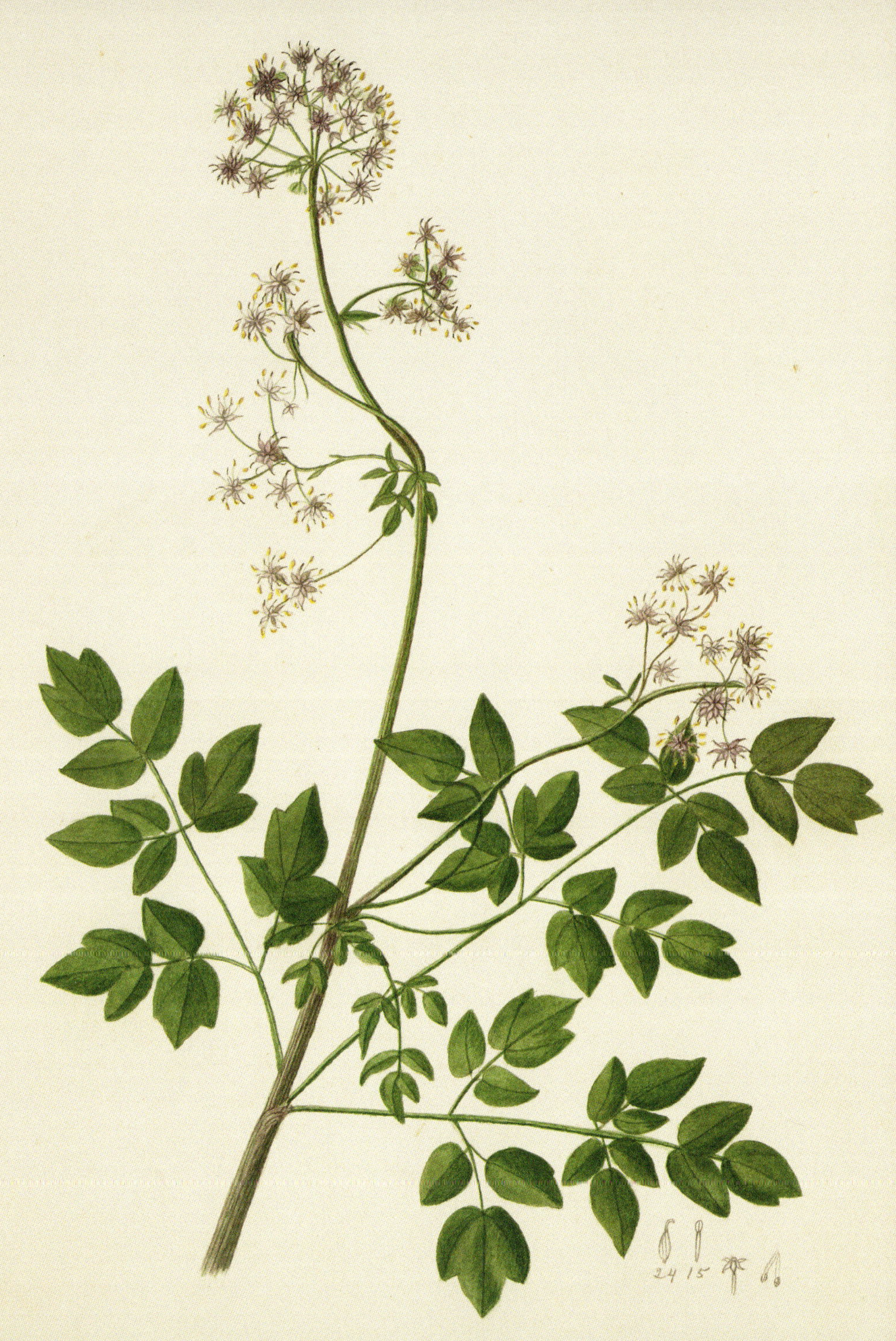
24 15

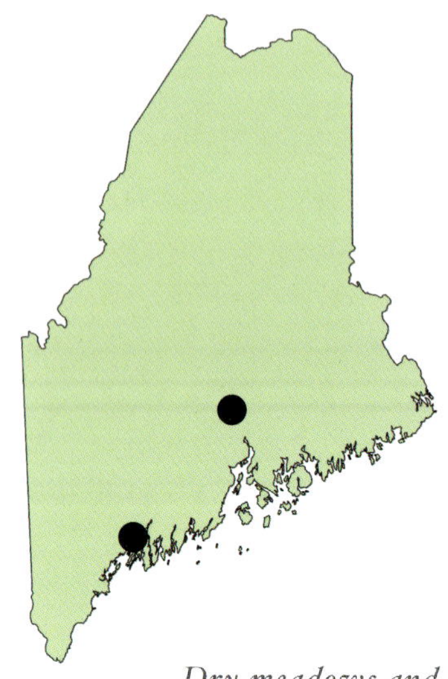

Dry meadows and grassy, rocky outcrops

Furbish Observed At:

Brunswick (1875)
Brewer (1880)

BULBOUS CROWFOOT

Ranunculus bulbosus

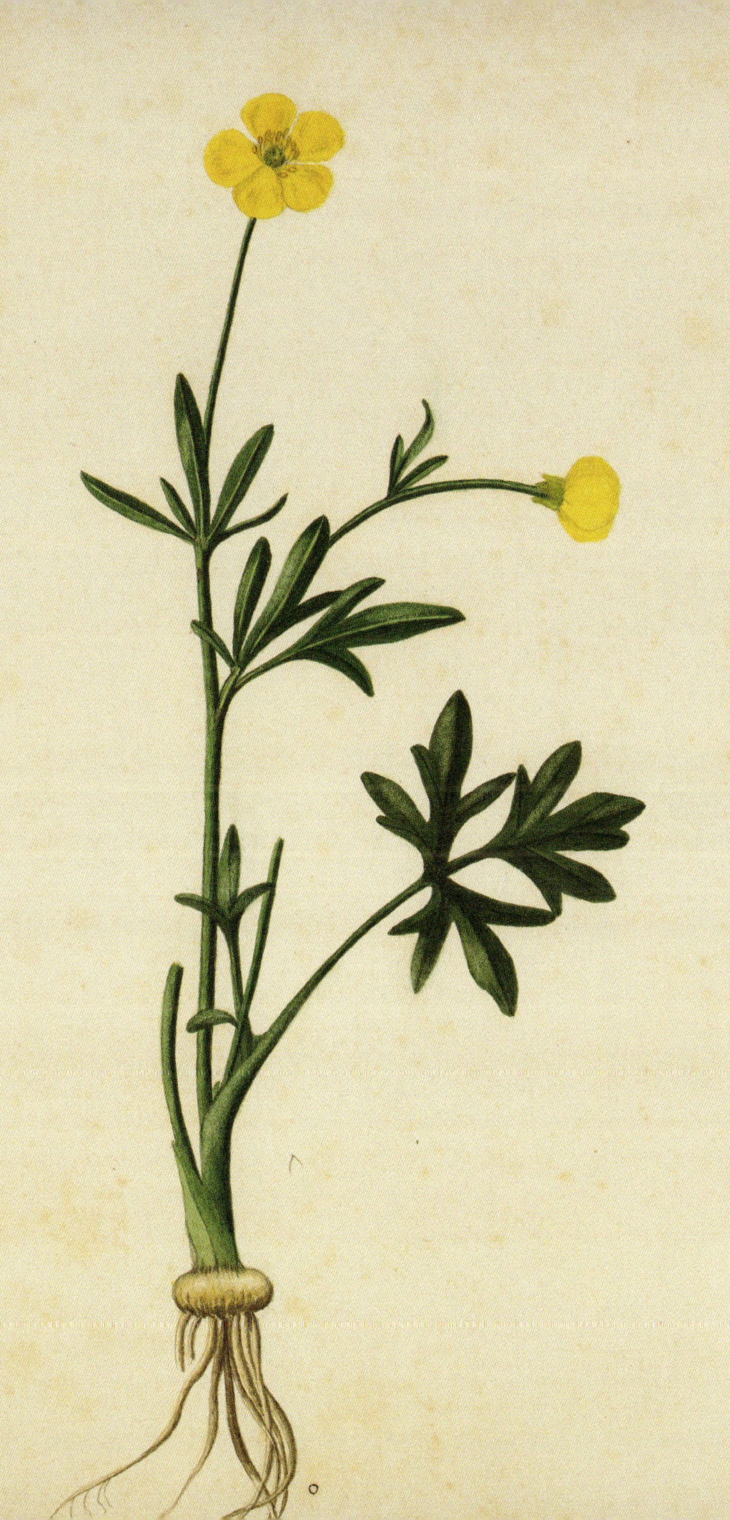

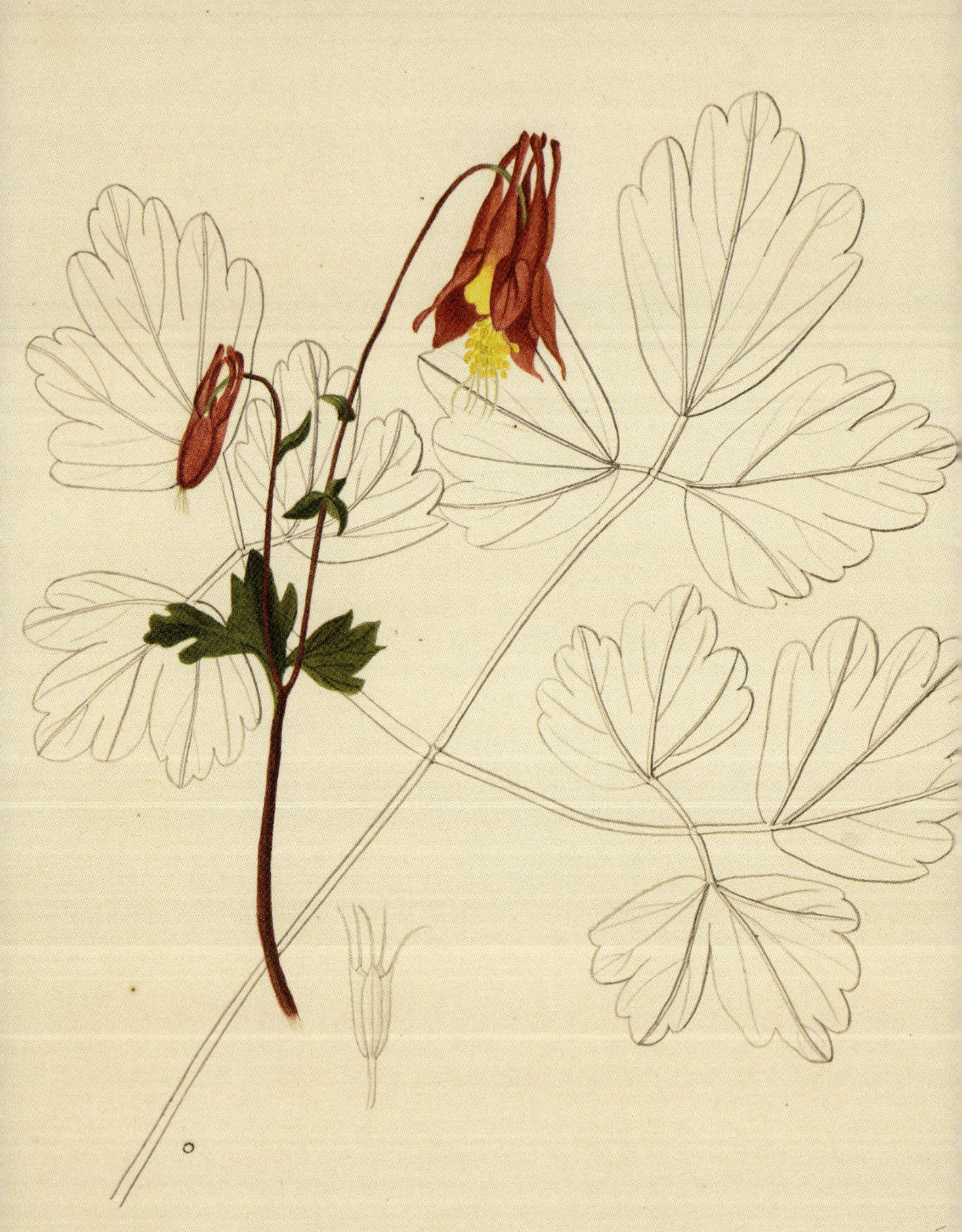

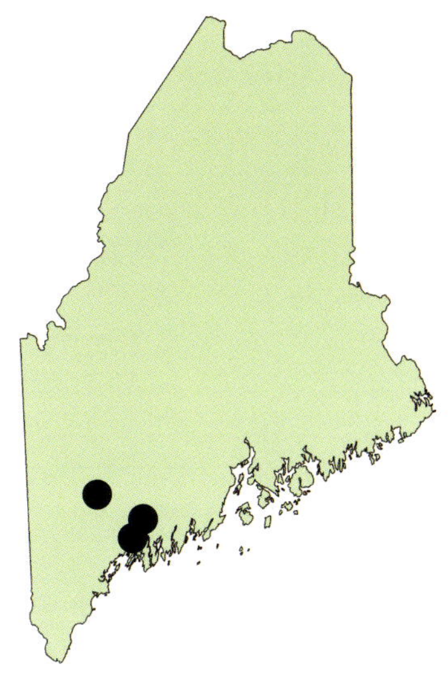

Ledges, cliffs, and rocky woodlands

Furbish Observed At:

Brunswick (1870)
Topsham (1870)
South Poland (1893)

RED COLUMBINE

Aquilegia canadensis

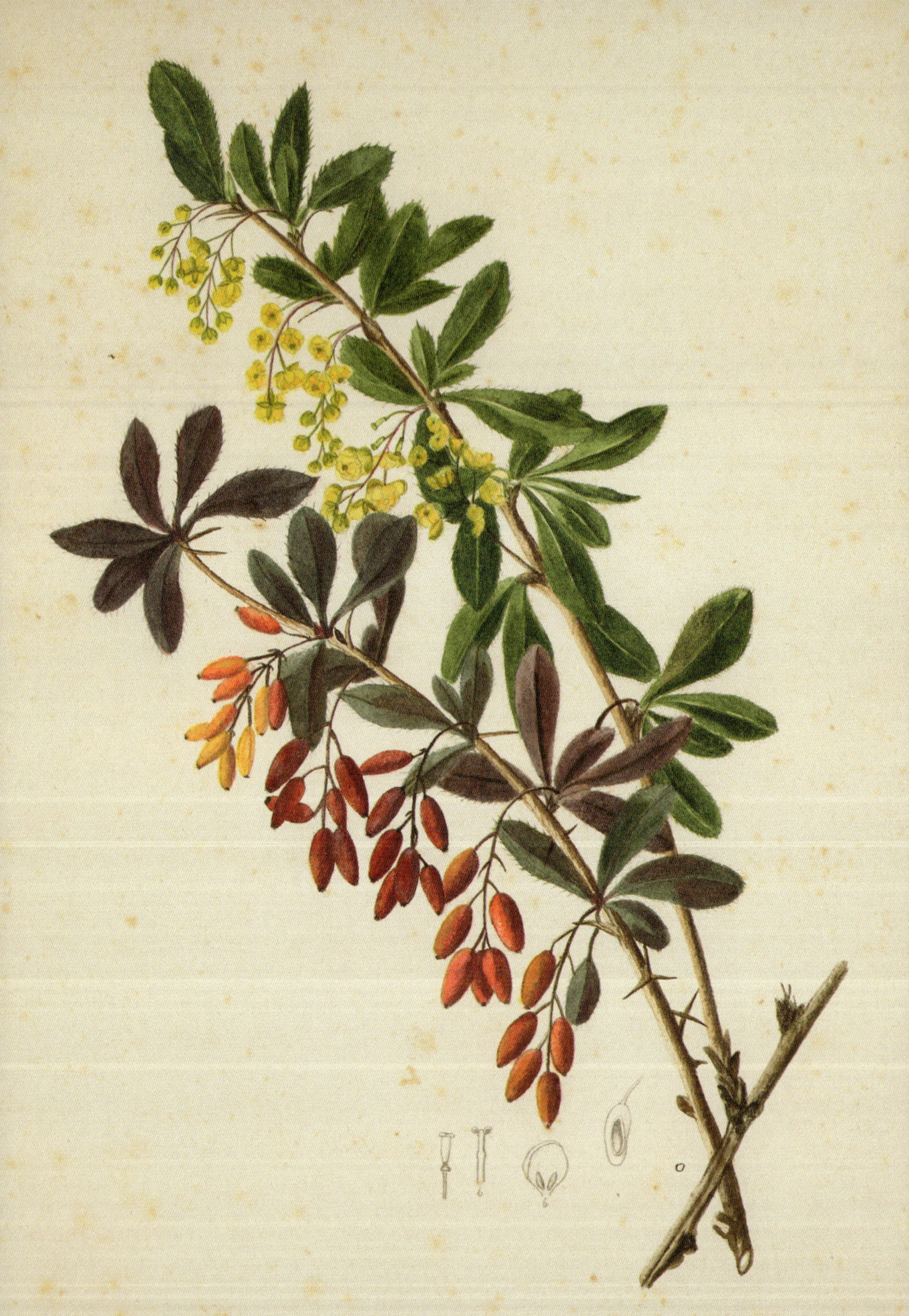

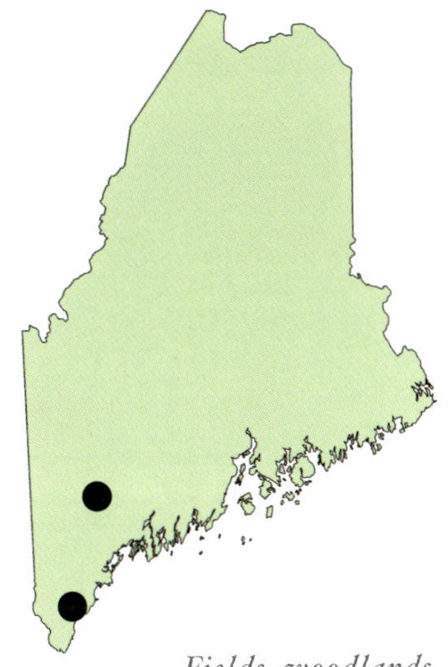

Fields, woodlands, and roadsides

Furbish Observed At:

South Poland (1896)
Wells (1898)

COMMON BARBERRY

Berberis vulgaris

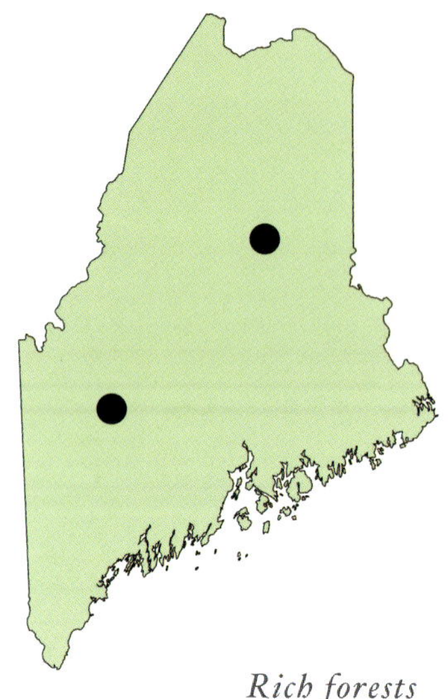

Rich forests

Furbish Observed At:

Patten (1881)
Strong (1882)

DUTCHMAN'S BREECHES & SQUIRREL CORN

Dicentra cucullaria & Dicentra cucullaria

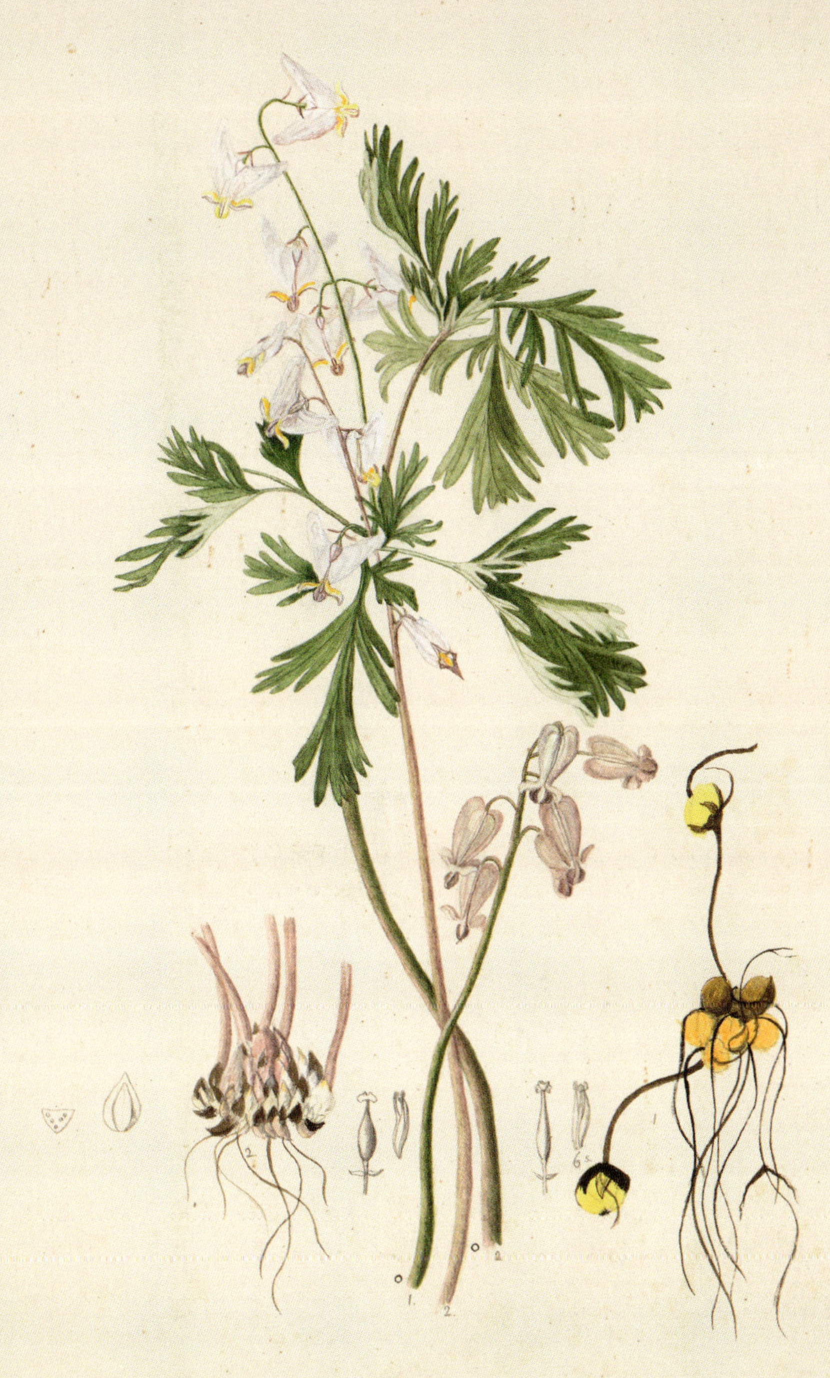

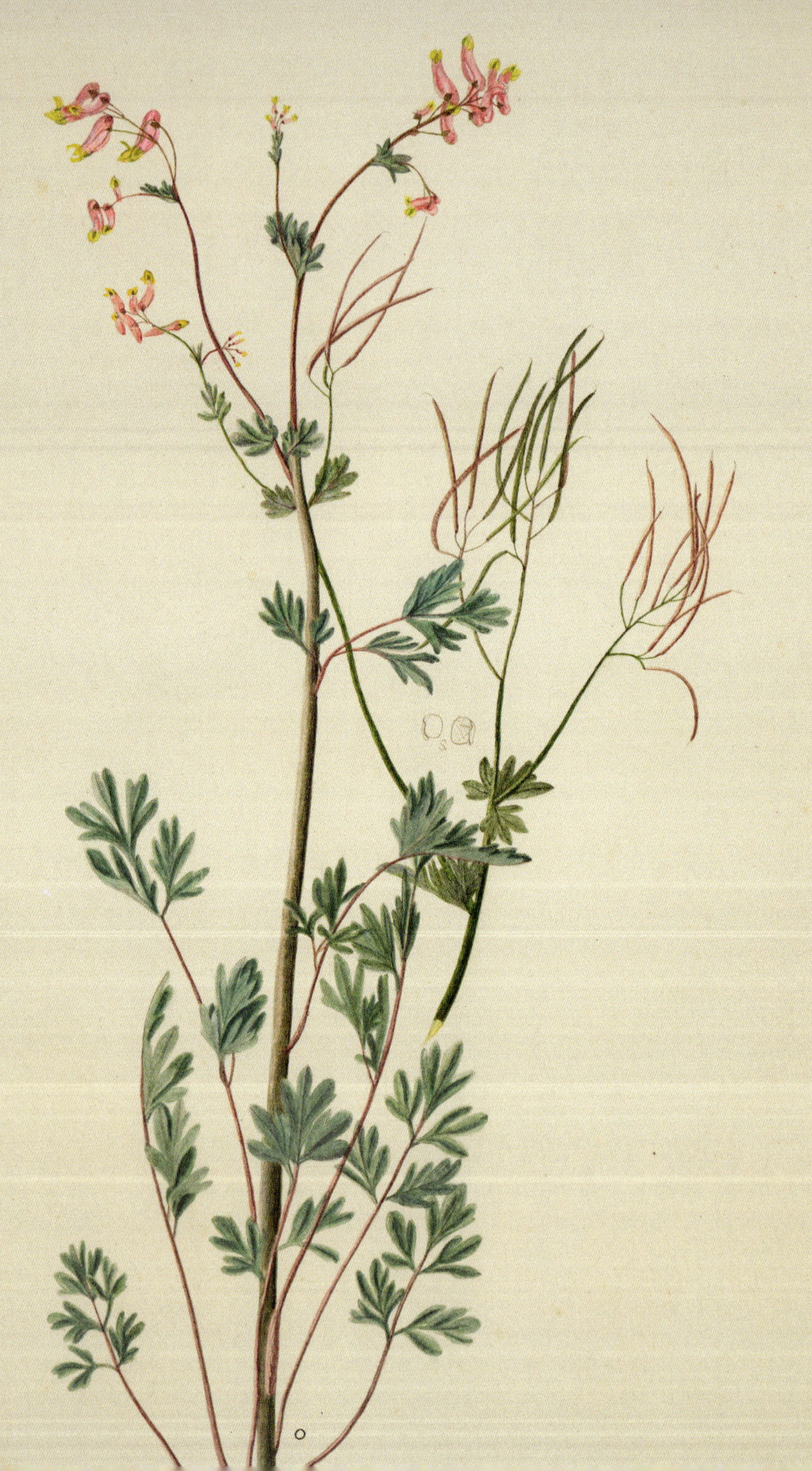

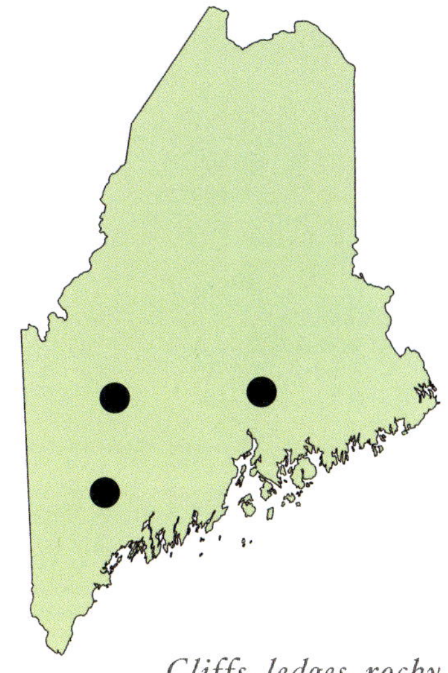

Cliffs, ledges, rocky woodlands, and clearings

Furbish Observed At:

Orono (1881)
Strong (1882)
South Poland (1893)

PINK CORYDALIS

Capnoides sempervirens

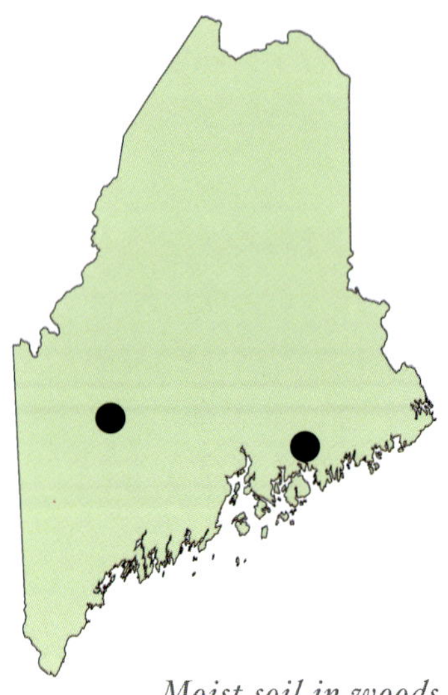

Moist soil in woods
and along stream banks

Furbish Observed At:

Avon (1882)
Franklin (n.d.)

HOBBLEBUSH

Viburnum lantanoides

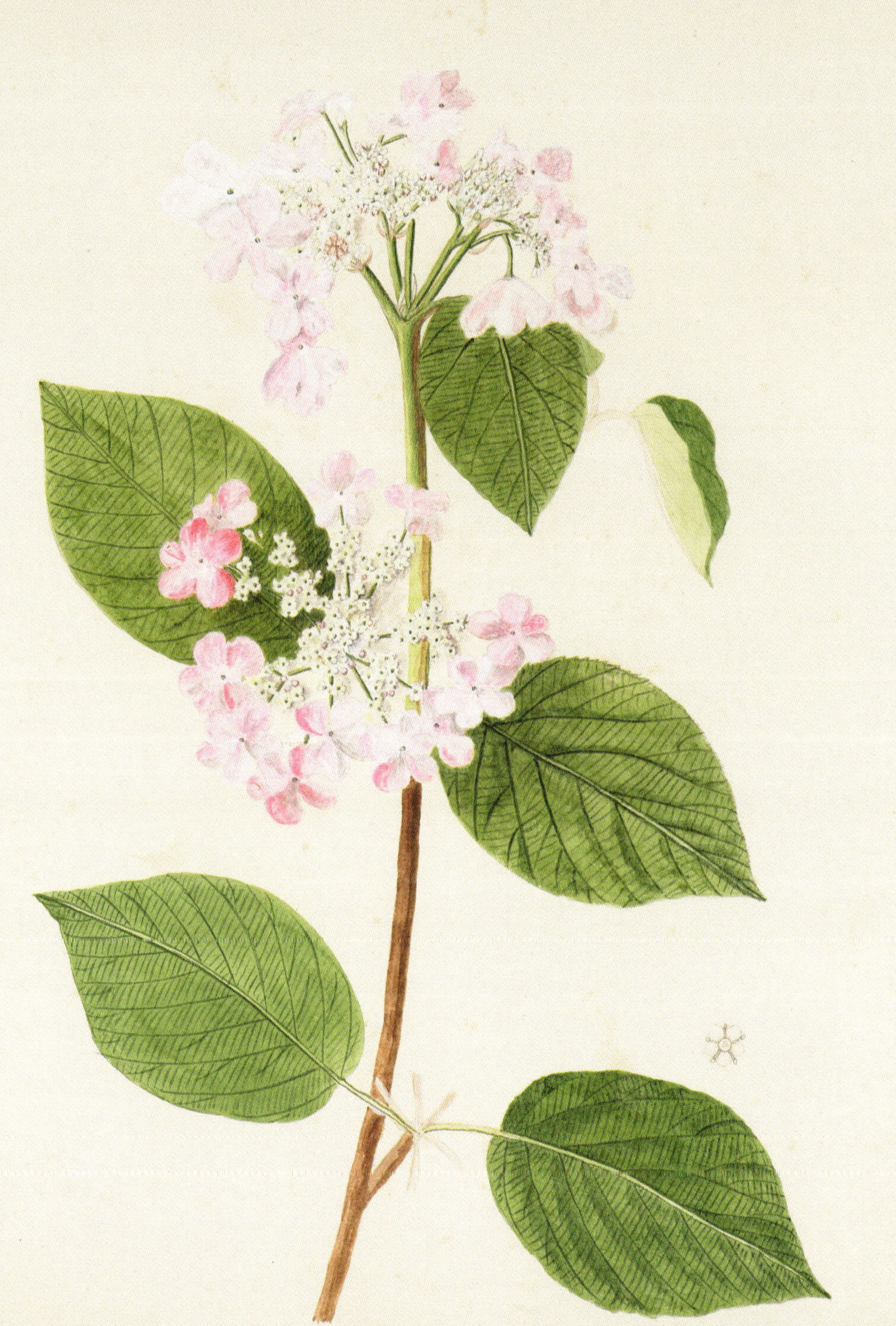

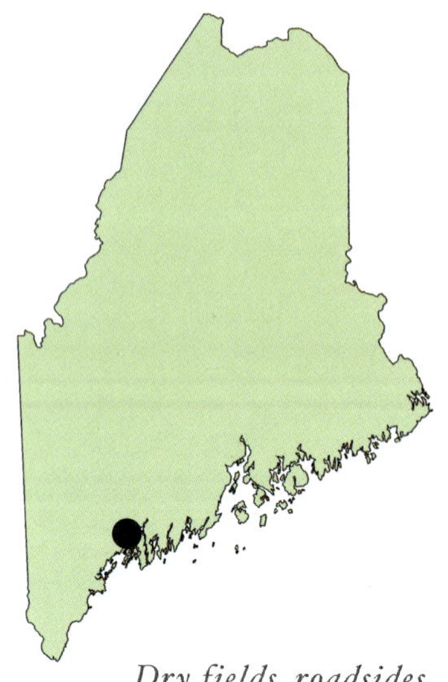

Dry fields, roadsides, and open banks

Furbish Observed At:

Brunswick (1903)

COMMON ST. JOHN'S WORT

Hypericum perforatum

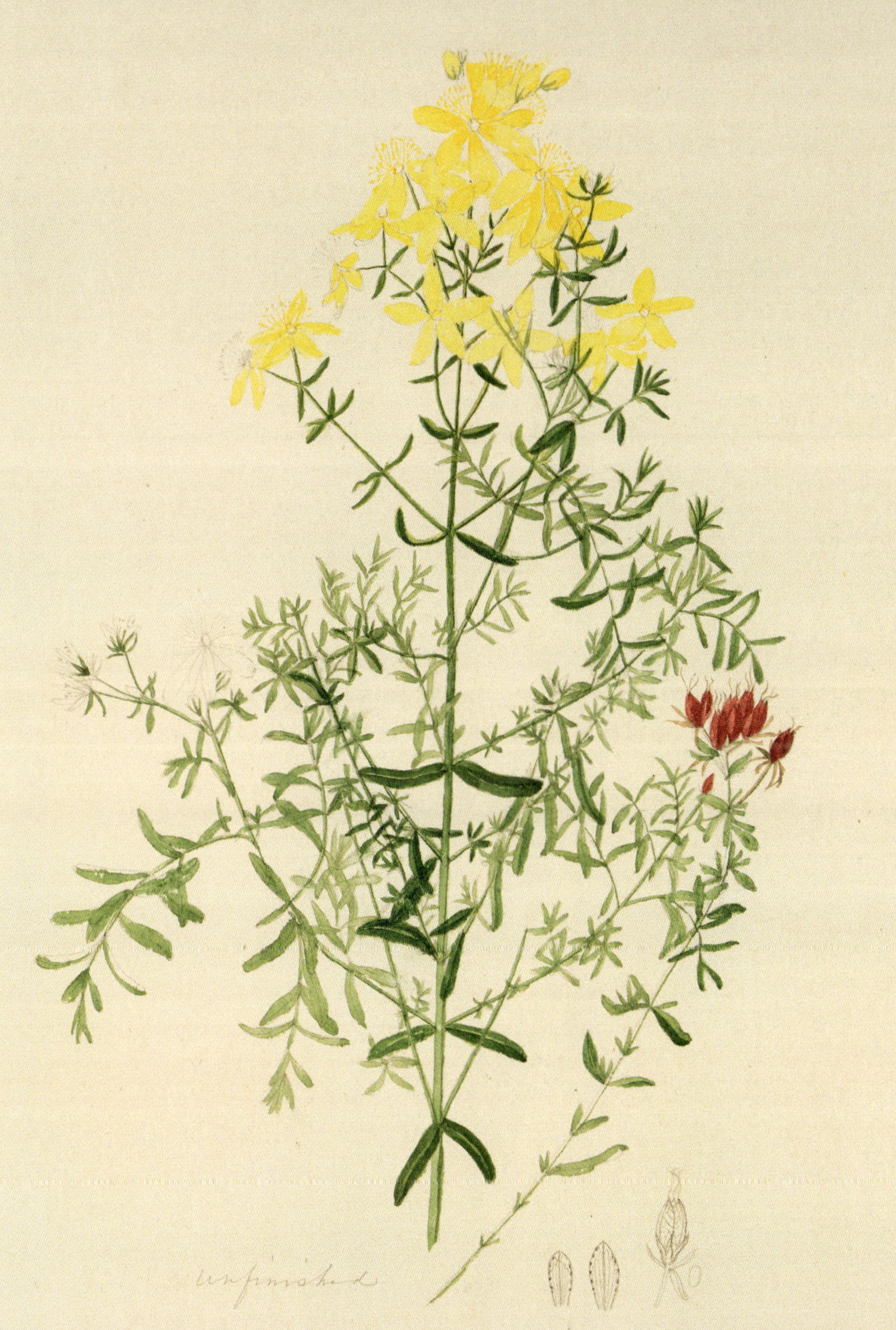
unfinished

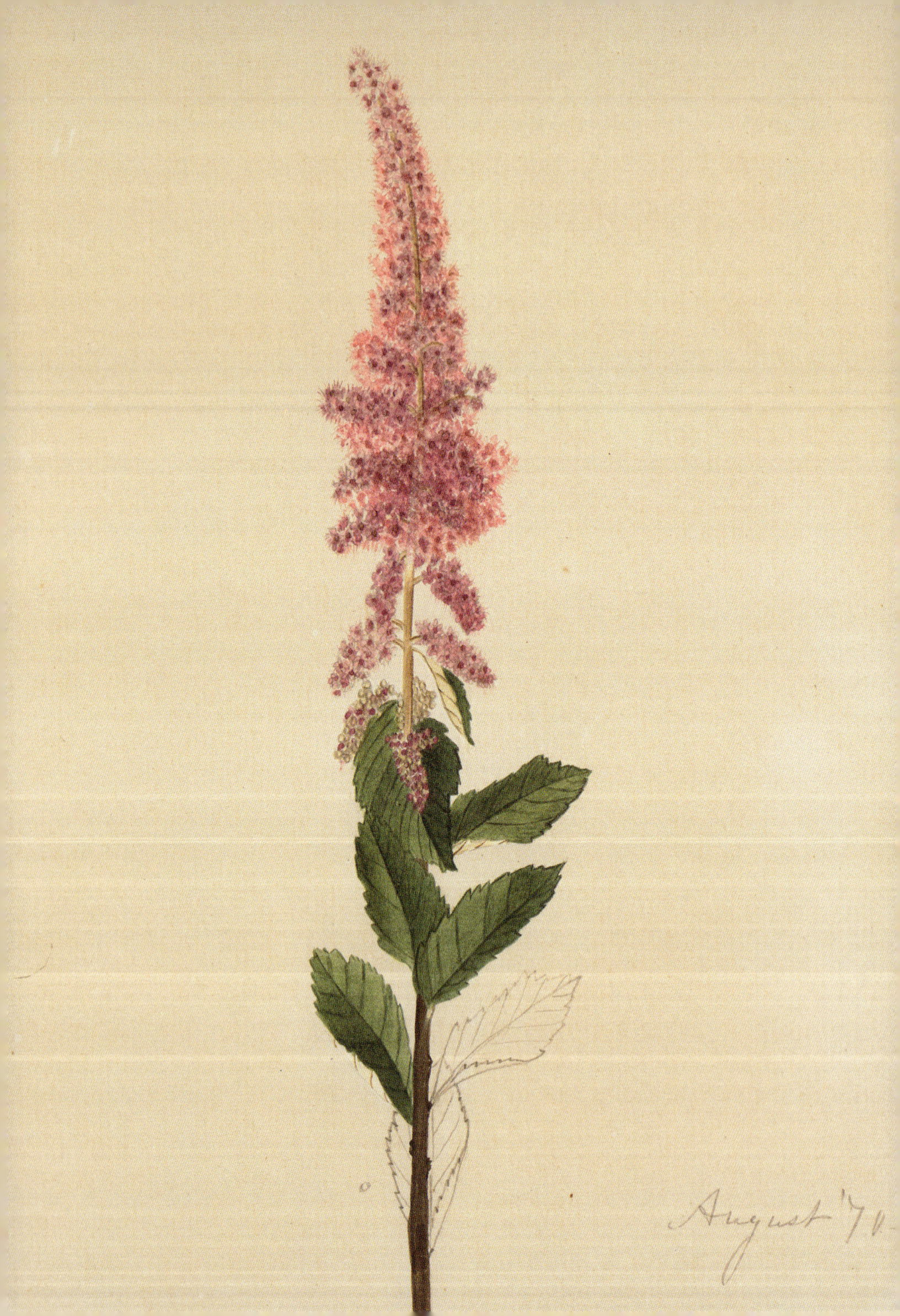
August '70.

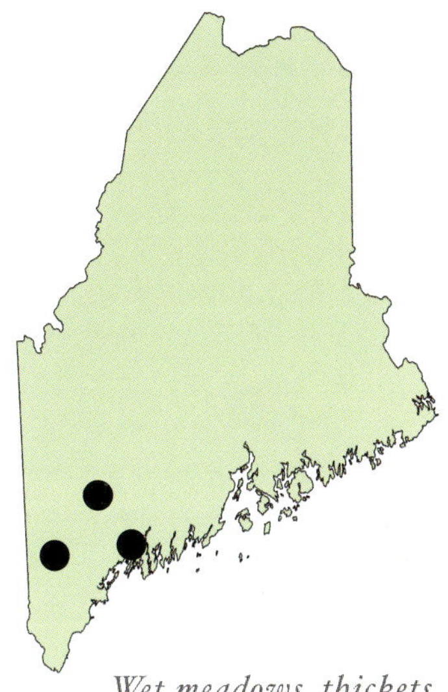

Wet meadows, thickets, and stream banks

Furbish Observed At:

Brunswick (1870)
West Baldwin (n.d.)
South Poland (n.d.)

ROSY MEADOWSWEET

Spiraea tomentosa

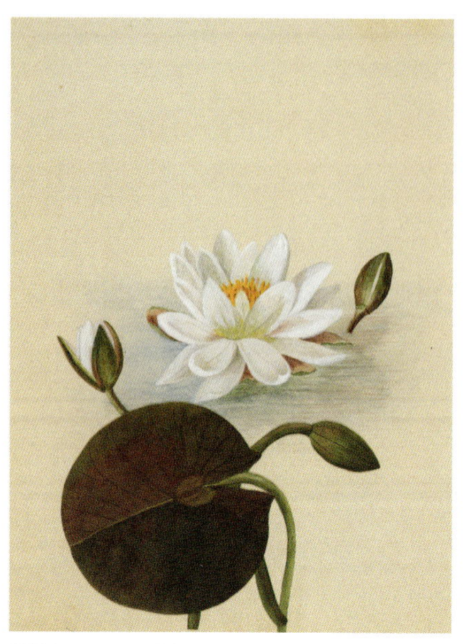

White water lily
(Nymphaea odorata)

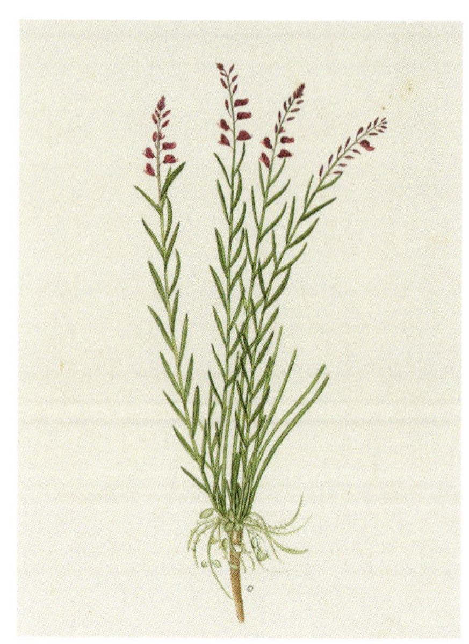

Racemed milkwort
(Polygala polygama)

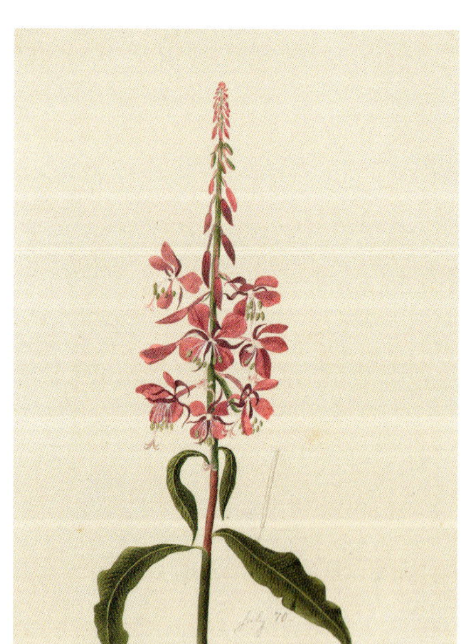

Narrow-leaved fireweed
(Chamerion angustifolium)

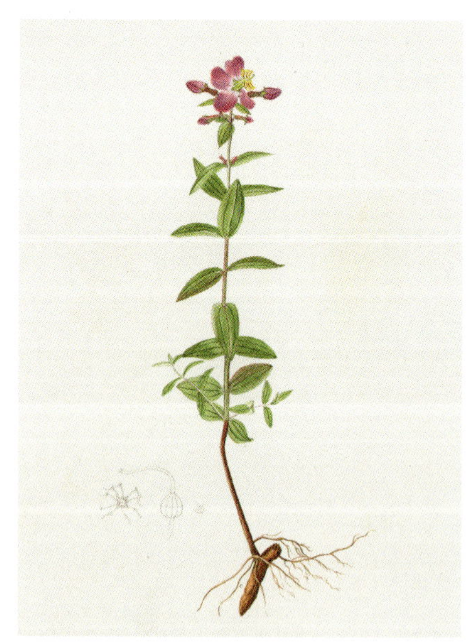

Virginia meadow-beauty
(Rhexia virginica)

In early 1873, Furbish lost both parents within a month and her collecting came to an abrupt halt.

During this difficult time of her life, Furbish took great comfort in her deep and abiding faith. She also took comfort from her large network of friends within botanical circles. One of her first botanical friends was Anne Jackson, also from Brunswick, who "conferred with her on problems of identification" and helped add plants to her collection. Jackson also introduced her to George Edward Davenport, who would become her longtime friend and correspondent. Davenport, by trade a manufacturer of picture frames in Boston, shared Furbish's ardent interest in botany, but unlike Furbish, his particular interest was in ferns. He was well-connected in Cambridge and eventually became a founding member of the New England Botanical Club and made numerous contributions to its botanical journals.

Through Kate's correspondence with Davenport, beginning in 1875, we glimpse a rare view of the day-to-day details, frustrations, triumphs, and simple joys of her efforts. She continued their botanical correspondence actively for many years, seeking his advice and assistance in procuring specimens or confirming identifications, and offering to send him ferns and other plants in return. The letters show that during the late 1870s Furbish was hard at work and acquiring a great amount of experience in a diversity of taxonomic groups. Her herbarium collections, hitherto comparatively sparse, started to become more regular, with at least 1,000 surviving from 1876–1879.

With a decade of botanical experience behind her, and with the help and encouragement of friends and colleagues like Davenport and Jackson, Furbish was perfectly poised for the great northern adventure for which she is well remembered.

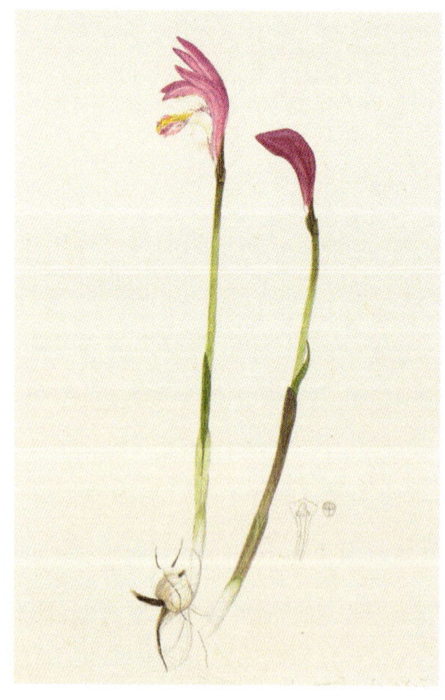

Dragon's mouth
(Arethusa bulbosa)

In 1880, Furbish embraced adventure and travelled far beyond her usual botanical haunts to collect species from areas in Maine she had not yet visited. A primary goal was to visit the northern and eastern areas of Aroostook County, which are underlain by shale and limestone bedrock. As such, she expected to encounter a variety of species that, restricted to the special growing conditions of those areas, she had not had the opportunity to study. With the enthusiasm and anticipation familiar to all botanists embarking into new territory, she planned her excursion with care.

On her way north, she spent some weeks in Orono, where she explored and collected a mix of common native, naturalized, and rare species, such as corn chamomile, yellow rocket, dragon's mouth, winterberry, and Kalm's lobelia, among many others. Her stop in Orono was also notable in that she met six-year-old Merritt Lyndon Fernald, son of the president of the Maine State College of Agricultural and the Mechanic Arts (now the University of Maine.) Fernald would later become her friend and Fisher Professor of Natural History at Harvard.

At that time, the journey into Aroostook was an adventure in itself, requiring travel first by train and then by carriage. Her immediate destination was Fort Fairfield, where she spent six weeks and found "to my delight the banks of the Aroostook River abounding in work for my brush." She made sketches of many plants she had not encountered before, including sticky tofieldia and marsh arrow grass. From there she continued along the Aroostook to Caribou and Presque Isle, where she forayed into cold bogs and other "wild and fascinating" places.

In the two and a half months I spent in this country, I noted 208 different plants, and added fifty new ones to my own list.

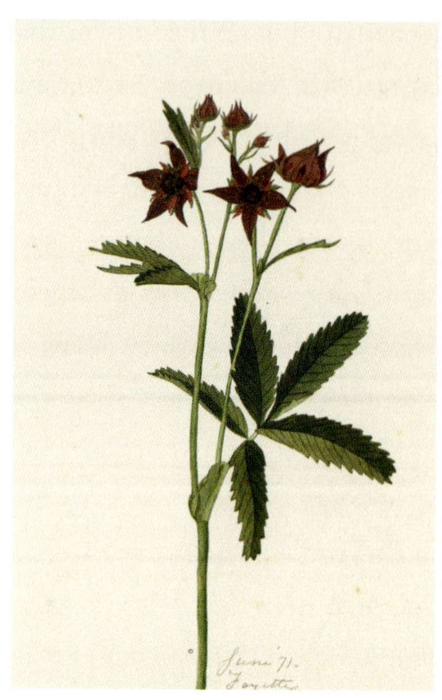

Marsh cinquefoil
(Comarum palustre)

In the winter following this first trip north, she wrote and sent sketches to her friend George Davenport, one of which was a lousewort. The plant was new to her so she also sent specimens for study to the esteemed Sereno Watson at Harvard. She later wrote to him to accept an invitation to visit him at the college and also in regards to the lousewort. As it turned out, the flower (now widely known as Furbish's lousewort) was a new species and Davenport suggested that it be named after Furbish. This specimen and many of her original specimens still reside in the collections of the Gray Herbarium and the New England Botanical Club Herbarium at Harvard.

The following year, 1881, Kate returned to the region, taking the railroad north from Orono to botanize the Mattawamkeag River before travelling by stage to Patten, where she spent a week and left with "16 new sketches and a large packet of pressed plants." She then "staged it to Ashland." At that time the area was a veritable wilderness, with but few scattered homes and logger's cabins along the way; however at Ashland she noted that people were "hospitable and refined." In her week spent there she was happy to see a few new plants.

From there she traveled north to Fort Kent on a corduroy road via Portage and Eagle Lakes. With a flair for the dramatic, Furbish described how her driver "took out his pistol to load it, saying that he had been fired upon twice in two years, and might need to use it before Fort Kent." The interesting plants she observed at Fort Kent, situated at the confluence of the Fish and St. John Rivers, were too numerous to list, but she delved into the forested swamps in search of orchids, where she was "amply rewarded." She next visited the village of St. Francis, where she found additional treasures, such as bottle gentian. Even her return trip home was fruitful; she collected several notable grape ferns, and, at her last stop in Houlton, she observed two varieties of burdock.

Her great expedition had been a success, providing content for her first publications and associated lectures, and establishing her persona as an intrepid botanical explorer, endearing her to future generations of botanists.

On April 2, 1883, Furbish reached a high point of her botanical pursuits when she delivered a formal address to the Portland Society of Natural History. In addition to discussing her extensive fieldwork and her illustrations, she recounted in colorful detail the adventures—and mishaps—of her treks to the north woods and climbs in the western mountains.

After a long sojourn in Europe, Kate returned to Maine to resume her life's work in 1885. An exploration of Portland and its islands provided new coastal territory after her excursions into the northern and western reaches of Maine.

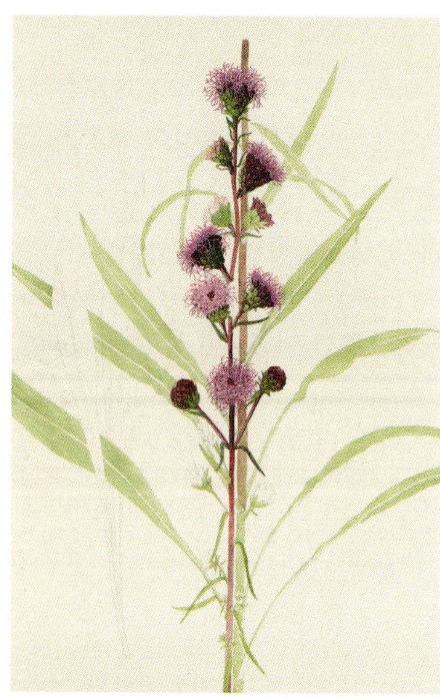

Northern blazing star
(Liatris novae-angliae)

Furbish re-entered a period of very intense productivity during the 1890s, the decade in which she turned sixty. Day by day, she continued to amass her growing botanical collection and to produce her impressive and still-growing collection of botanical illustrations.

In 1893, Furbish was appointed as botanist to the well-known Poland Springs House, calling into question the characterization of Furbish as merely an "amateur" botanist. Seen in this light, she was one of the first women professional botanists.

Kate set about creating a plant list and herbarium representative of the Poland area. Her duties also included creating a pamphlet for guests, many of whom were there to recover from illness, as well as engaging with and entertaining them. She seemed to thrive under her new professional duties and corresponded with her friend Merritt Lyndon Fernald, now at Harvard, about creating the herbarium, sending him specimens for the Harvard collection, as well. Her specimens from Poland endure to this day at The New England Botanical Club Herbarium (at Harvard), the Hodgdon Herbarium (at the University of New Hampshire), and the University of Maine Herbaria.

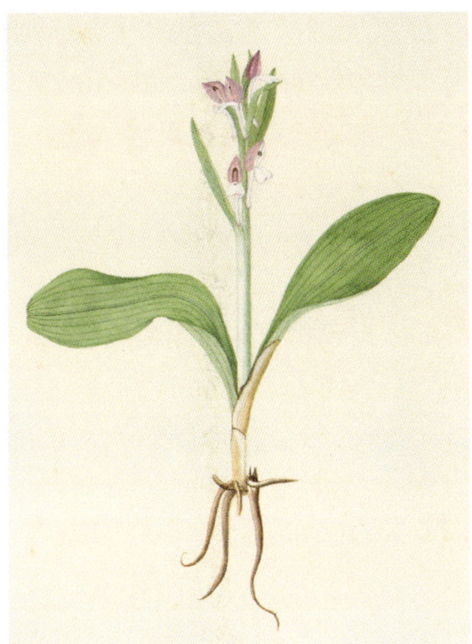

Showy orchid
(Galearis spectabilis)

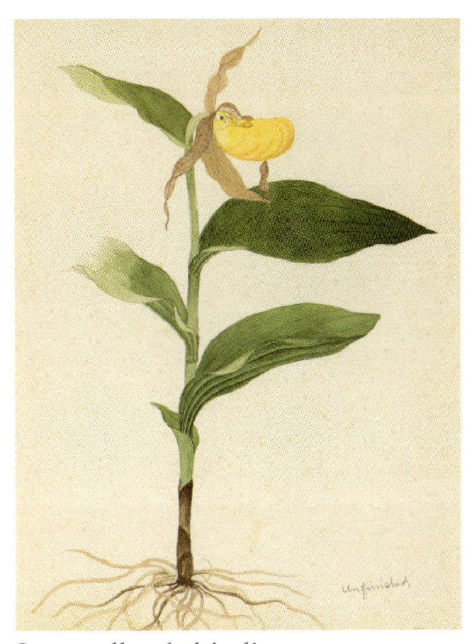

Large yellow lady's-slipper
(Cypripedium parviflorum var. pubescens)

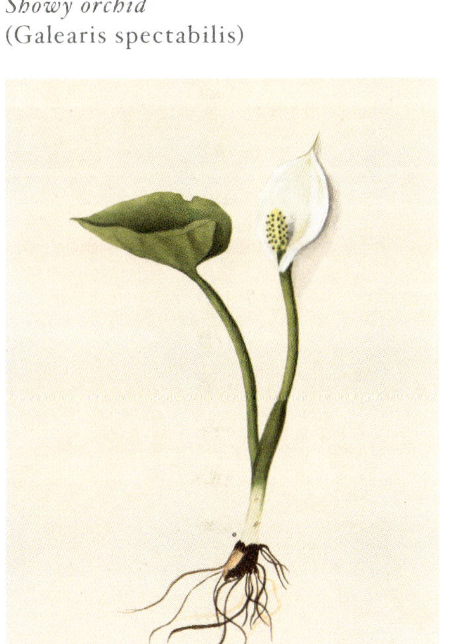

Wild calla
(Calla palustris)

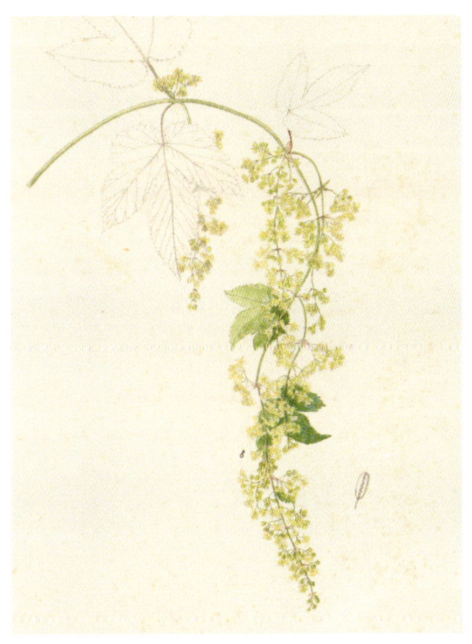

Common hops
(Humulus lupulus)

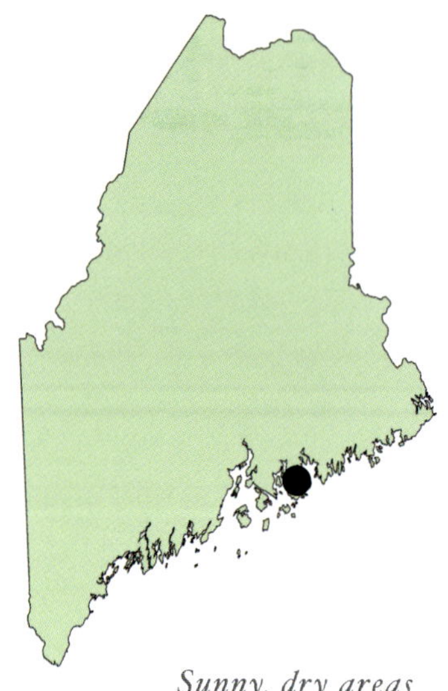

Sunny, dry areas and road sides

Furbish Observed At:

Mount Desert (1888)

SWEET-WILLIAM-CATCHFLY

Atocion armeria

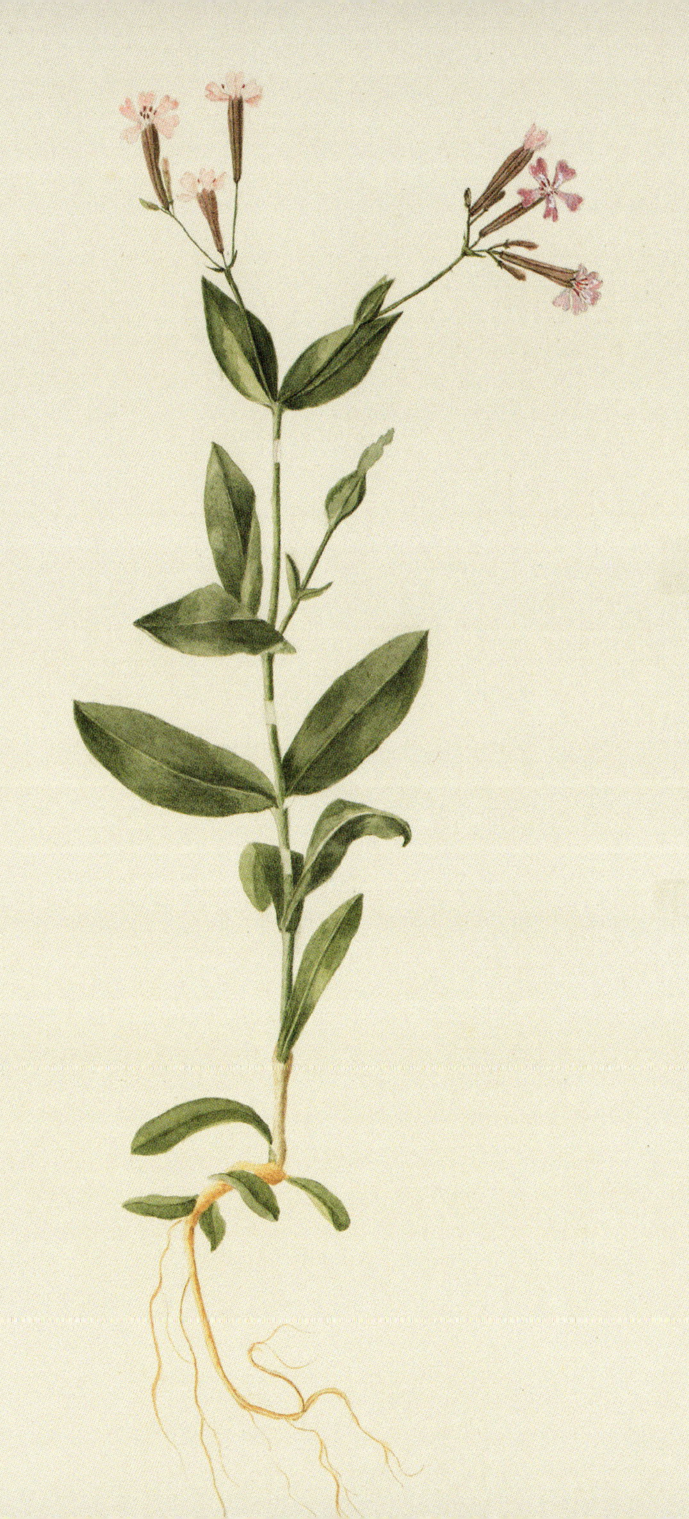

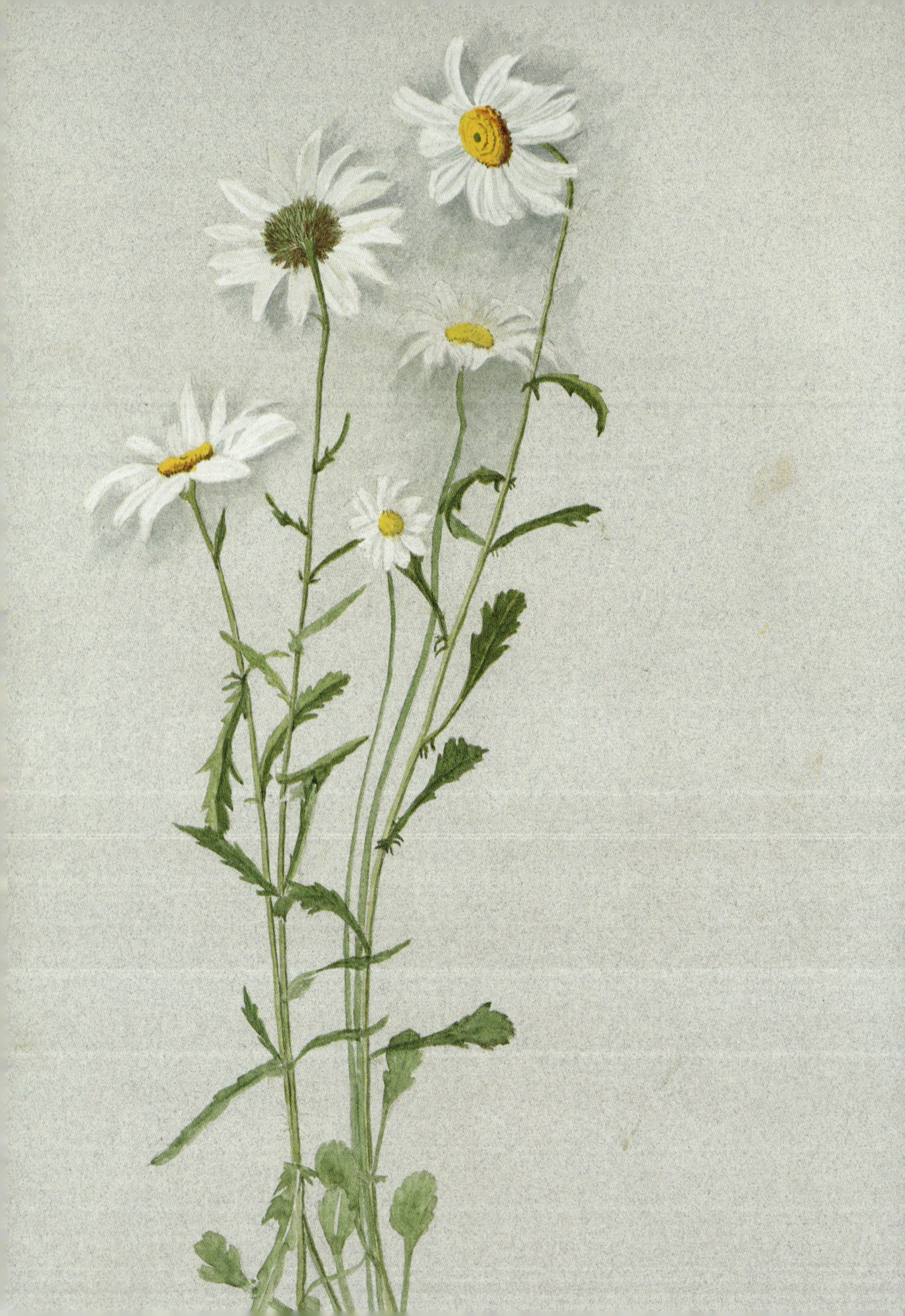

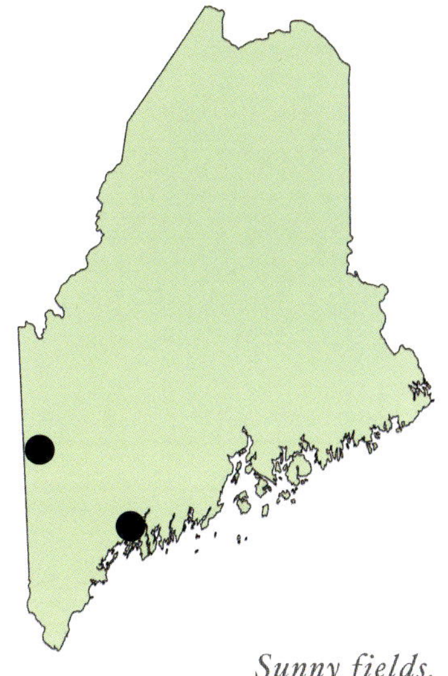

Sunny fields, roadsides, and meadows

Furbish Observed At:

Brunswick (1870)
Gilead (1897)

OX-EYE DAISY

Leucanthemum vulgare

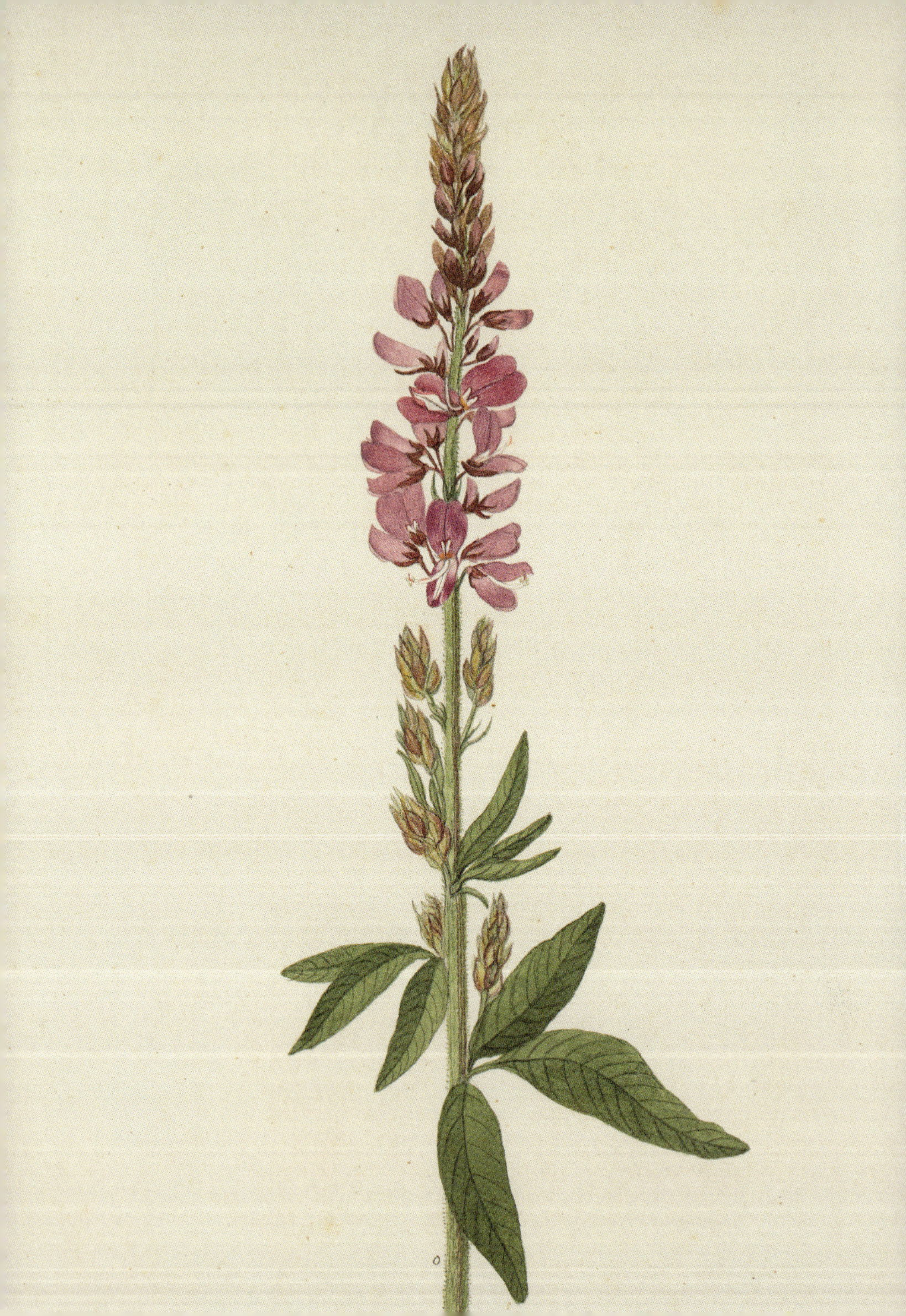

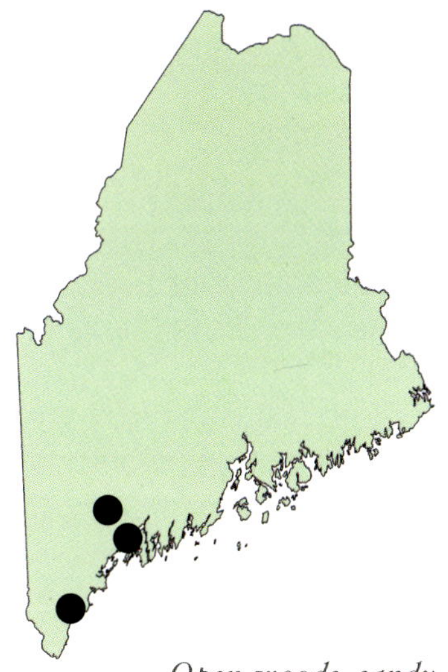

Open woods, sandy meadows, and roadsides

Furbish Observed At:

Brunswick (1870)
Wells (1879)
Lisbon Falls (1904)

SHOWY TICK-TREFOIL

Desmodium canadense

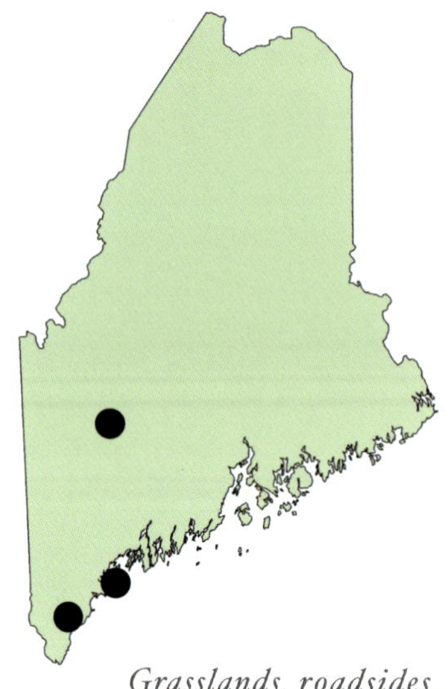

Grasslands, roadsides,
and forest clearings

Furbish Observed At:

Strong (1878)
Great Diamond Island (1893)
Wells (1898)

ORANGE HAWKWEED

Hieracium aurantiacum

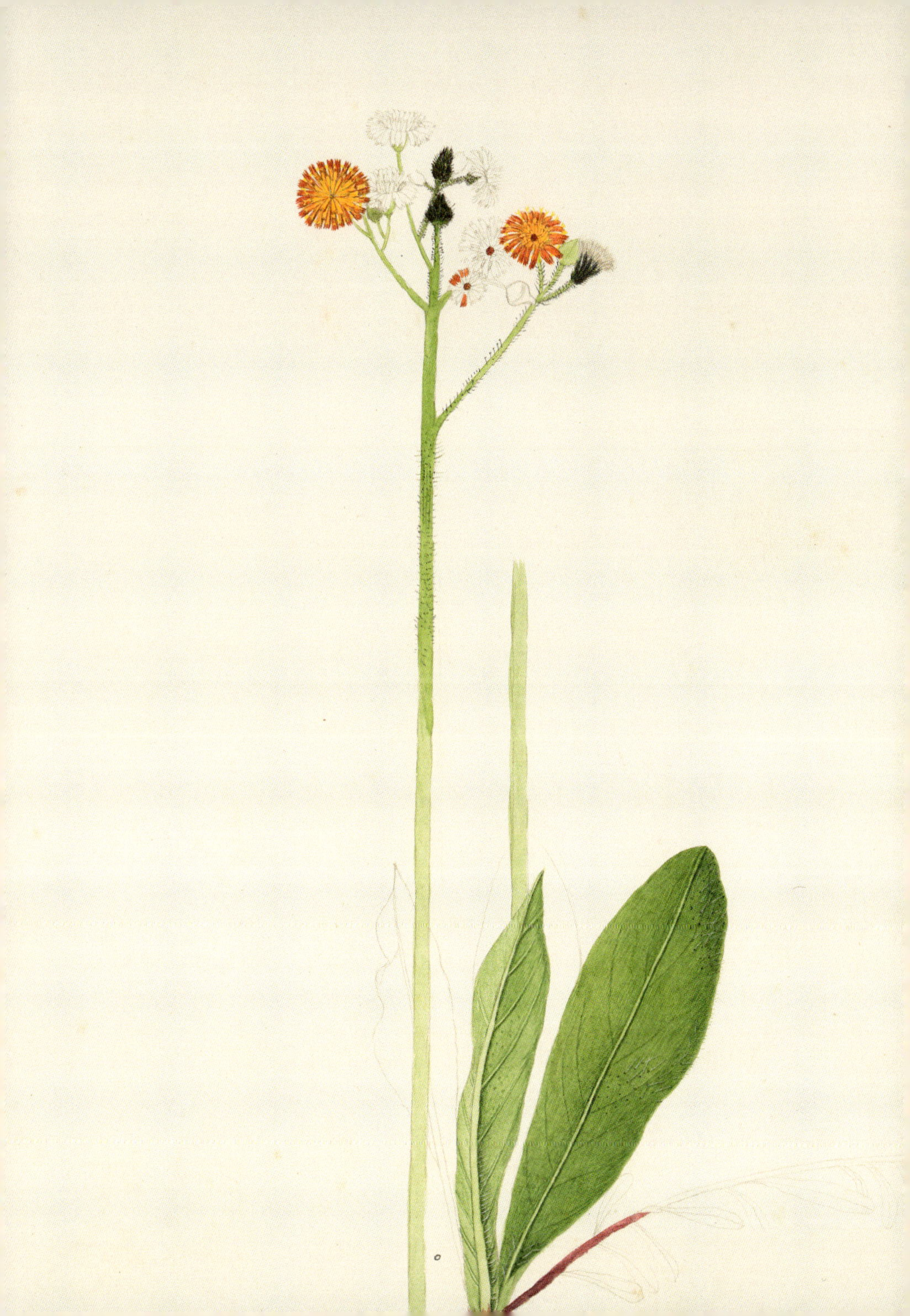

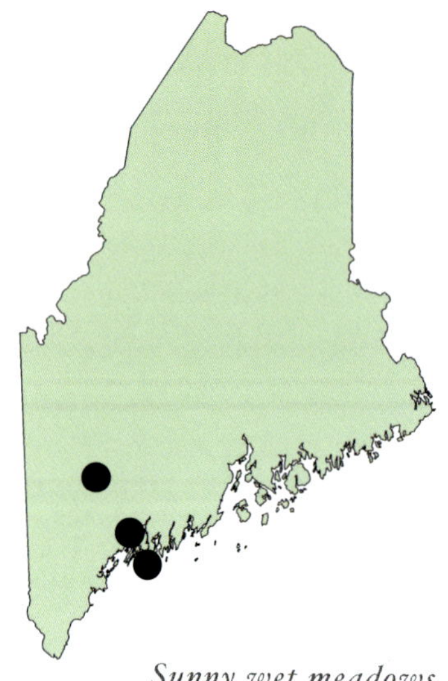

Sunny wet meadows and stream banks

Furbish Observed At:

Brunswick (n.d.)
Harpswell (n.d.)
South Poland (n.d.)

BLUE VERVAIN

Verbena hastata

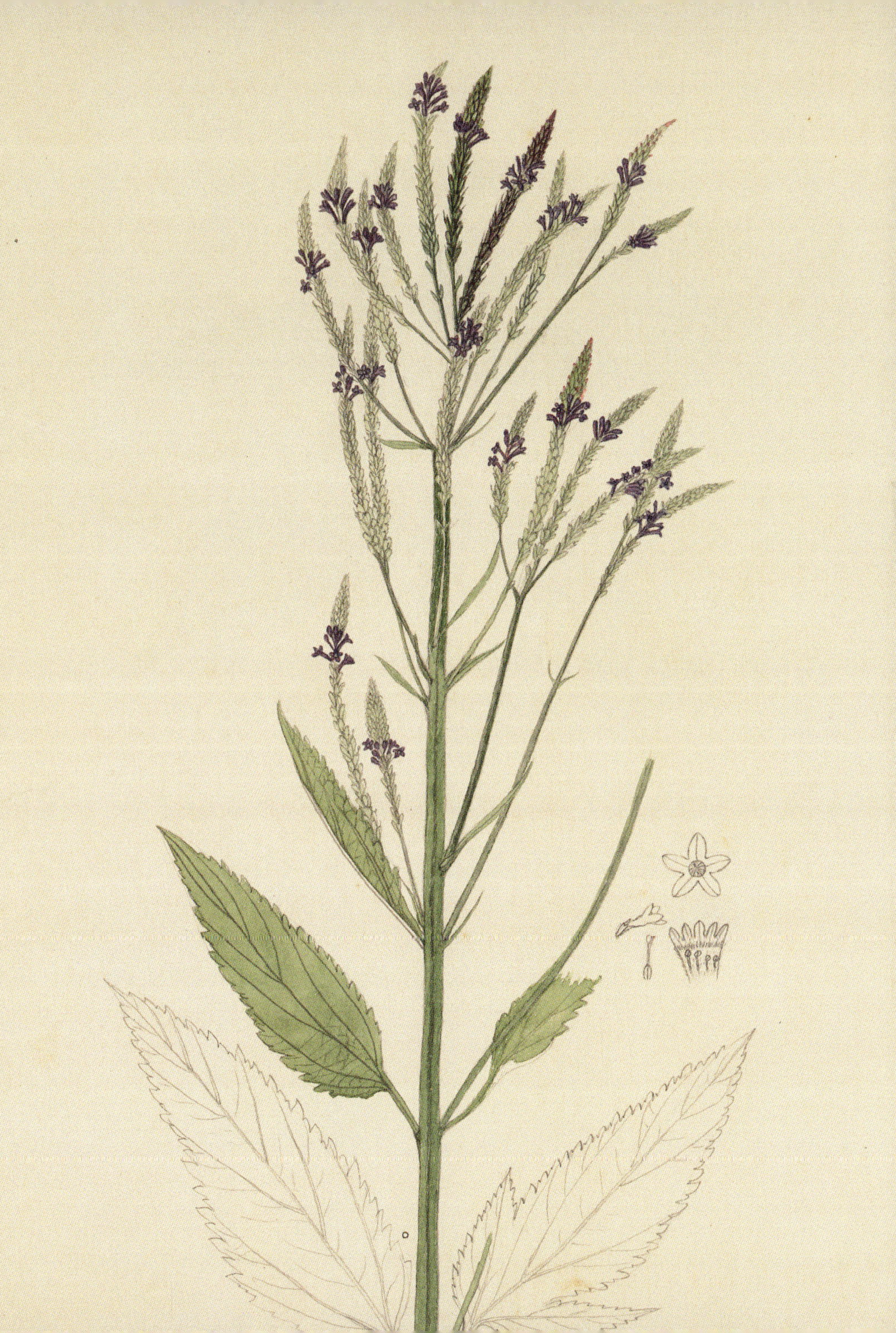

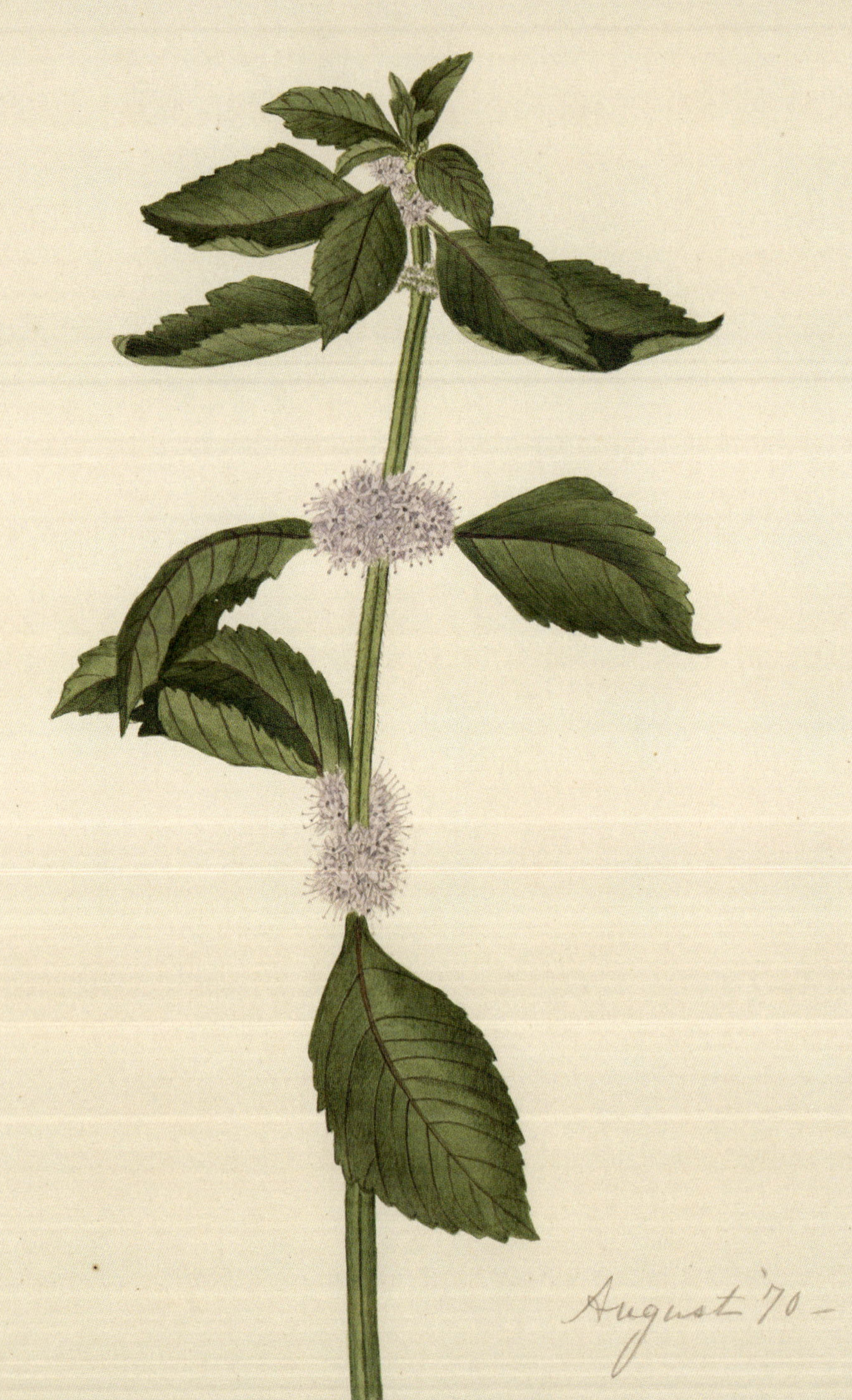
August '70 -

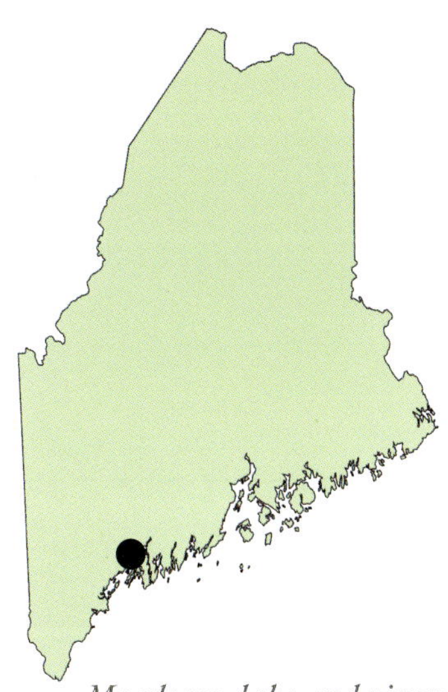

Meadows, lake and river fronts, and edges of wetlands

Furbish Observed At:

Brunswick (1870)

AMERICAN WILD MINT

Mentha canadensis

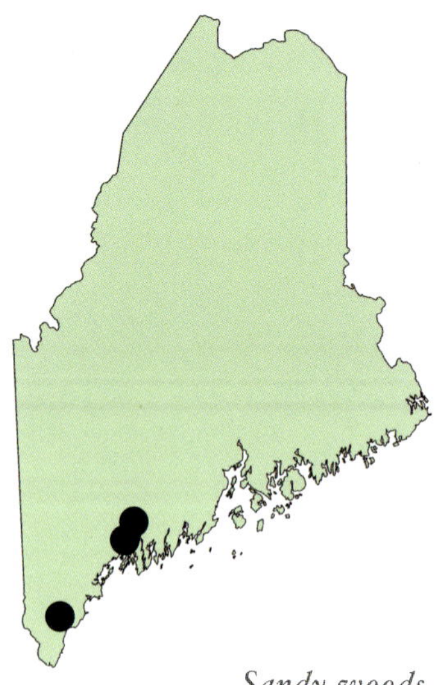

Sandy woods,
clearings, and banks

Furbish Observed At:

Brunswick (1870)
Topsham (1870)
Wells (1878)

TRAILING-ARBUTUS

Epigaea repens

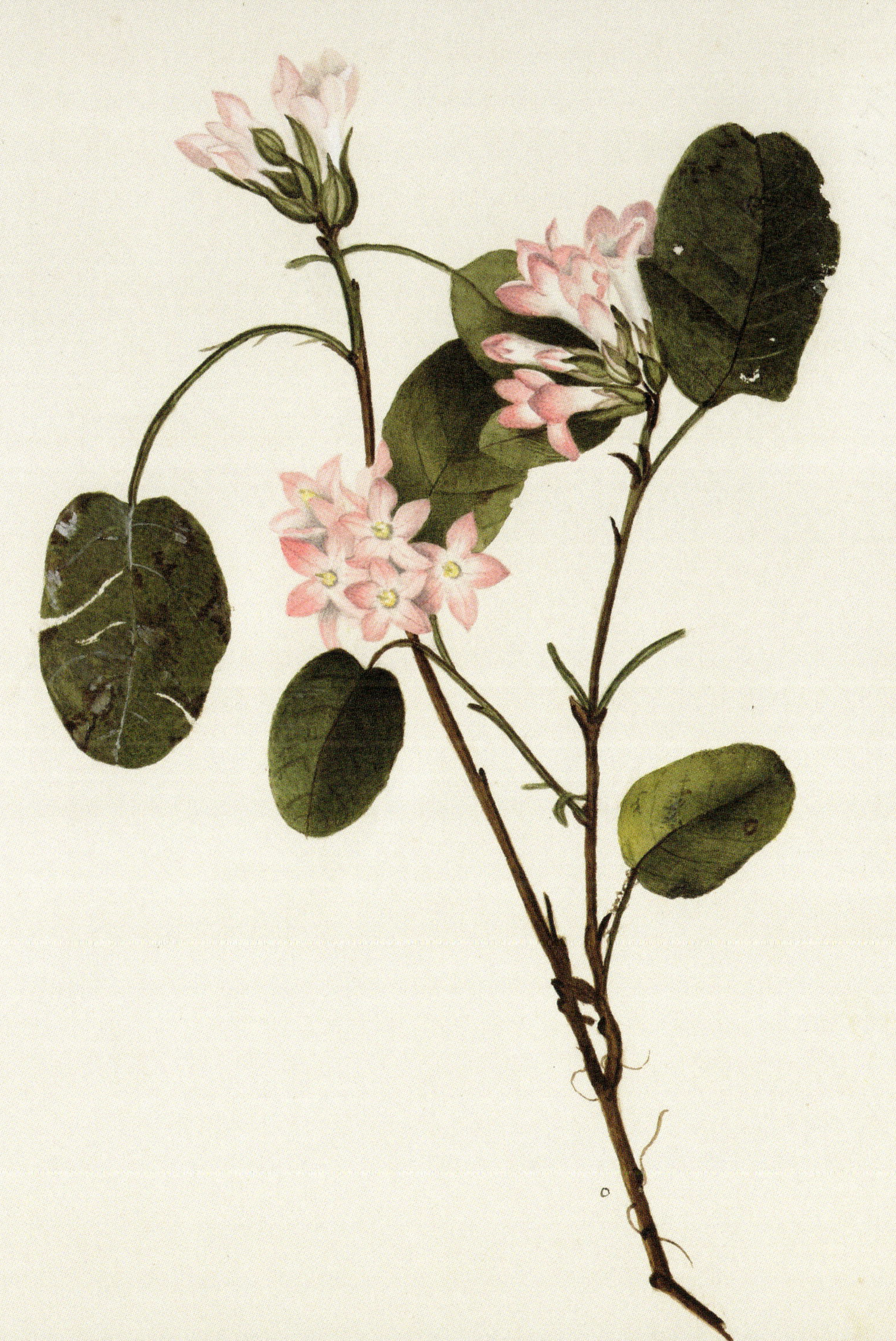

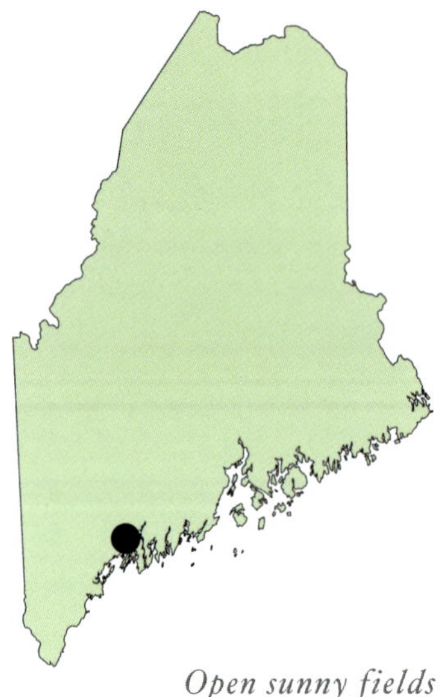

Open sunny fields and grasslands

Furbish Observed At:

Brunswick (1901)

COMMON DANDELION

Taraxacum officinale

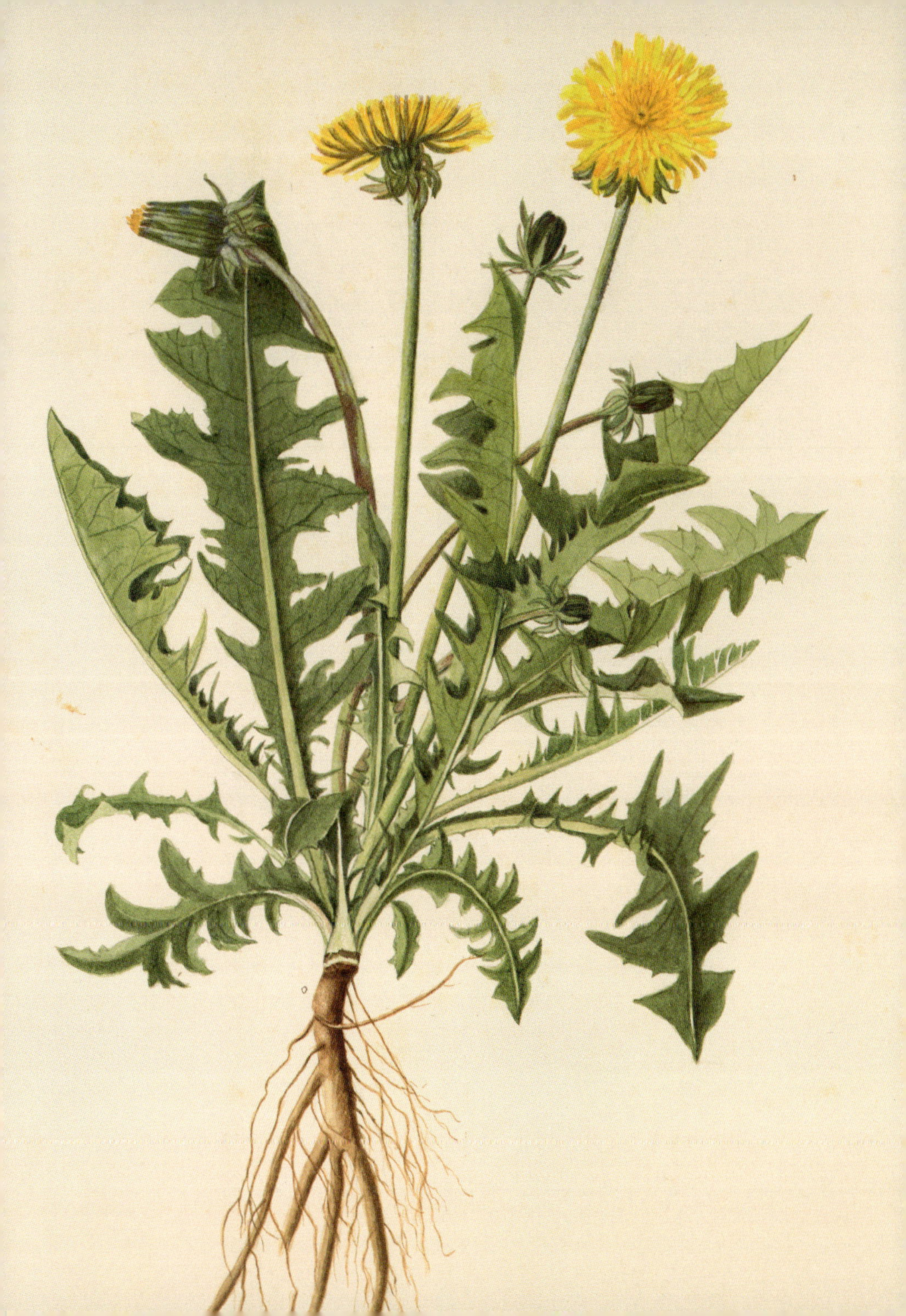

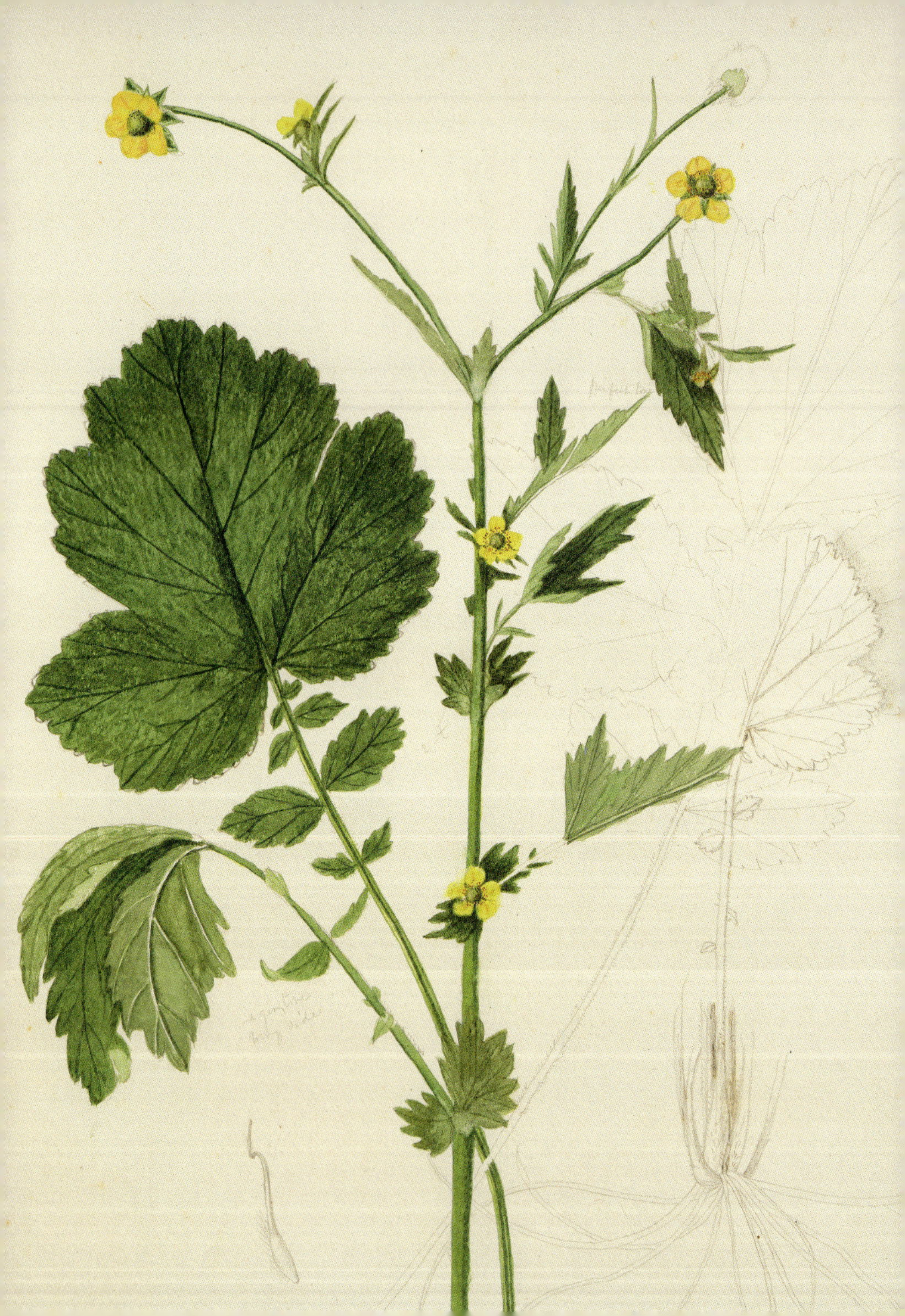

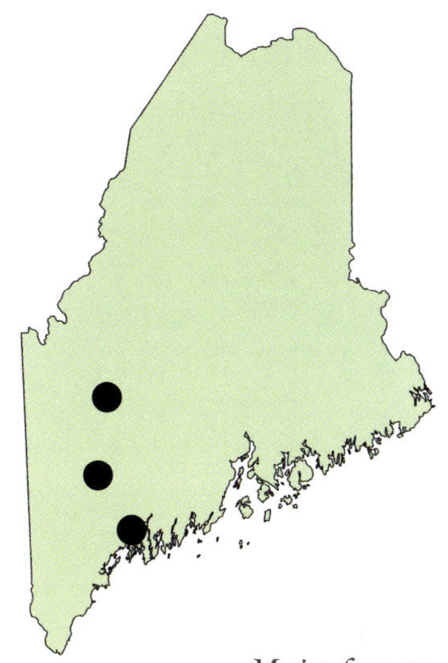

Moist forests,
swamps, and wetlands

Furbish Observed At:

Strong (1882)
South Poland (1893)
Brunswick (1904)

LARGE-LEAVED AVENS

Geum macrophyllum

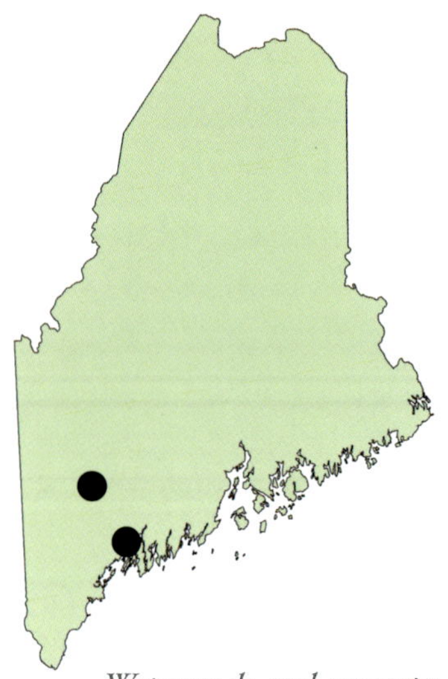

Wet woods and swamps

Furbish Observed At:

Brunswick (1870)
South Poland (1893)

JACK-IN-THE-PULPIT

Arisaema triphyllum

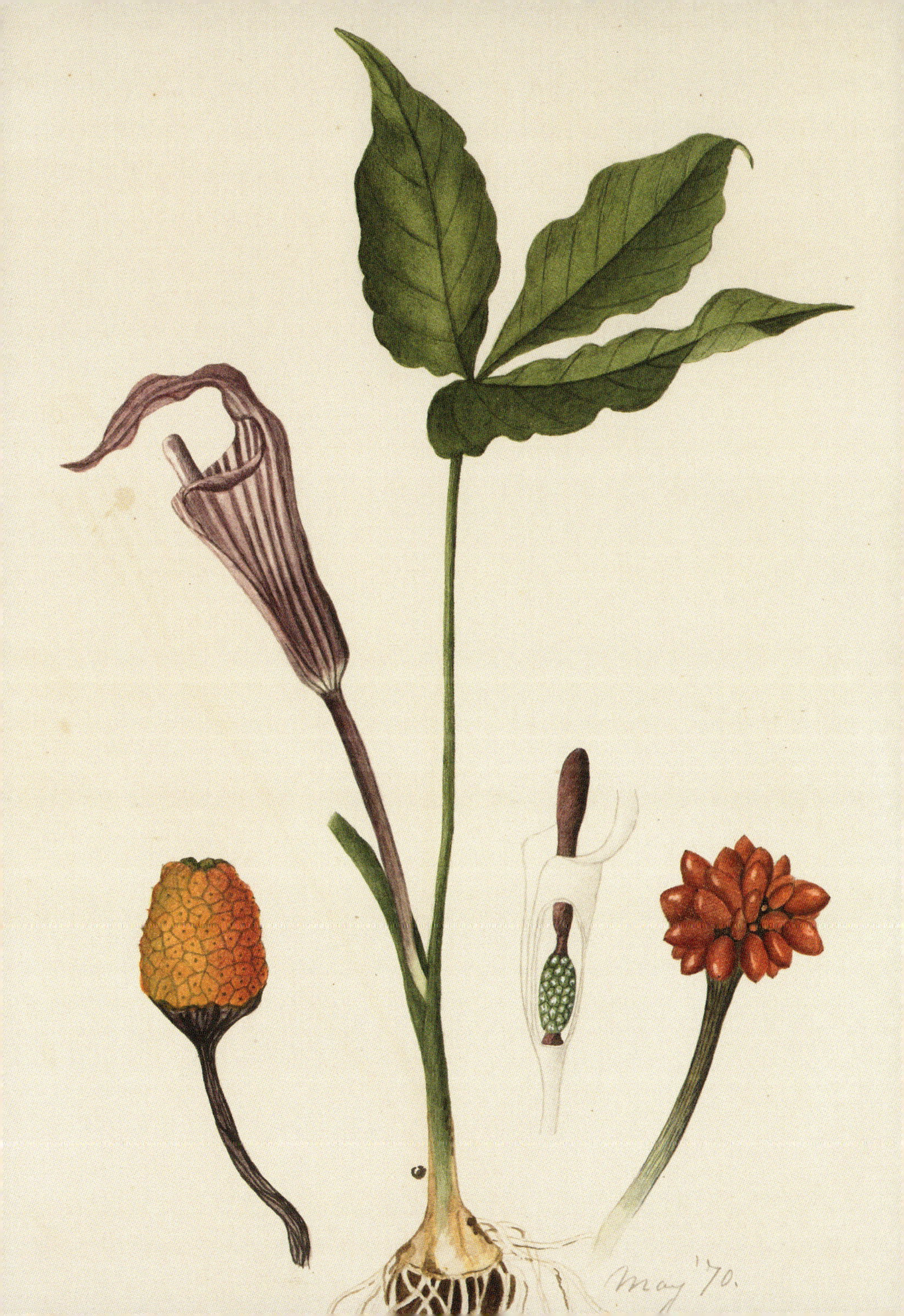
May '70.

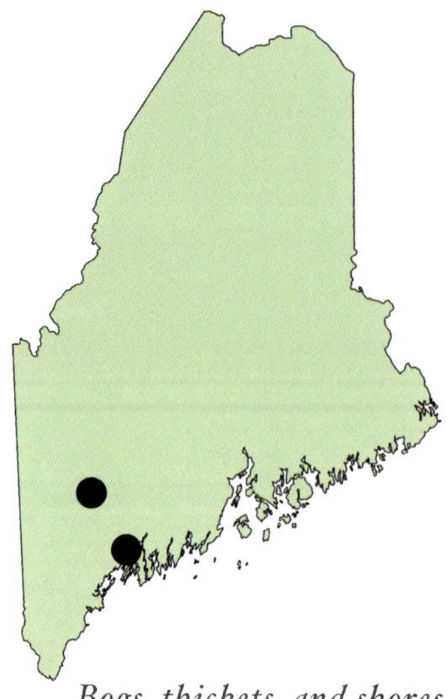

Bogs, thickets, and shores

Furbish Observed At:

Brunswick (n.d.)
South Poland (n.d.)

RHODORA

Rhododendron canadense

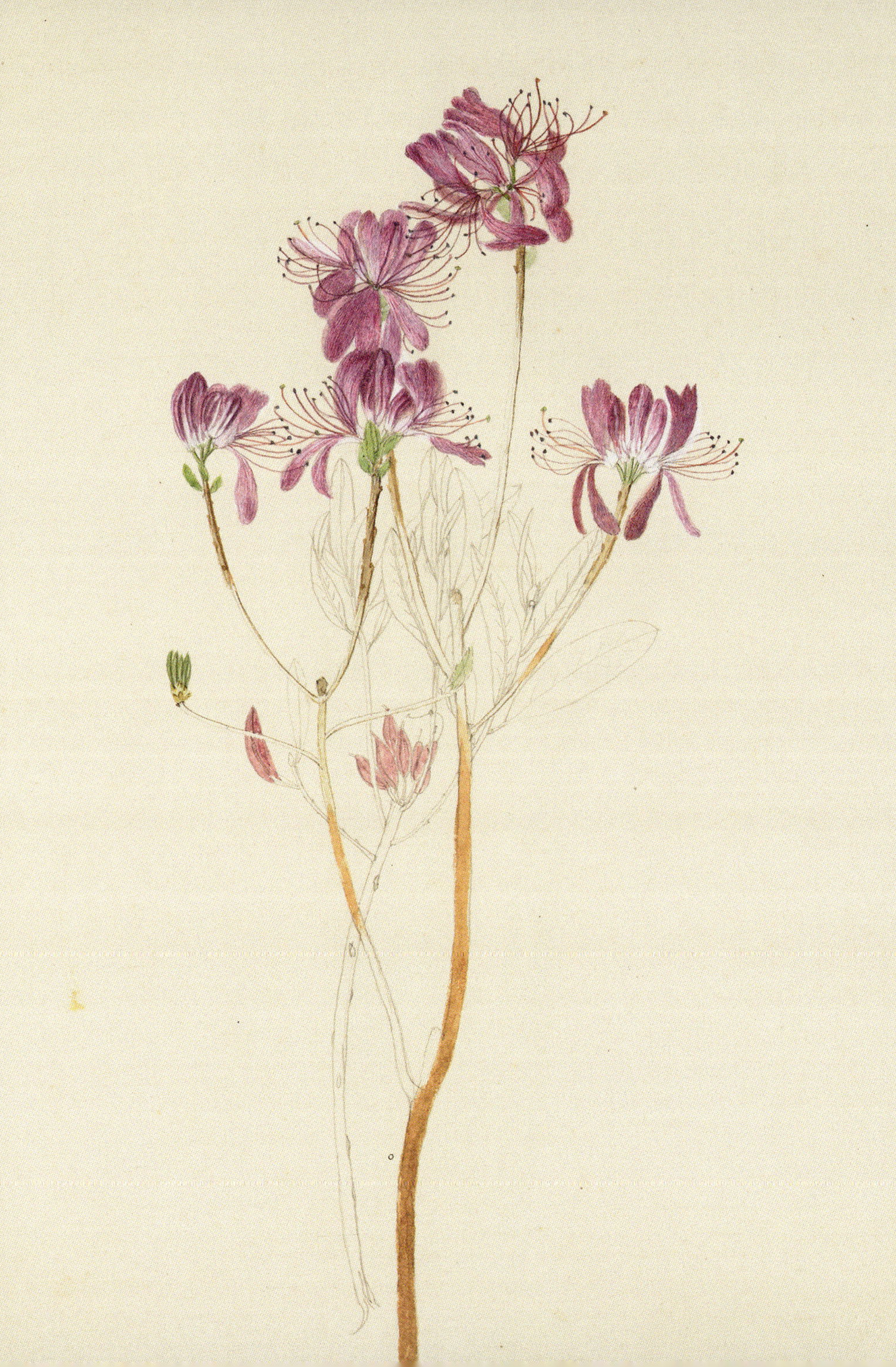

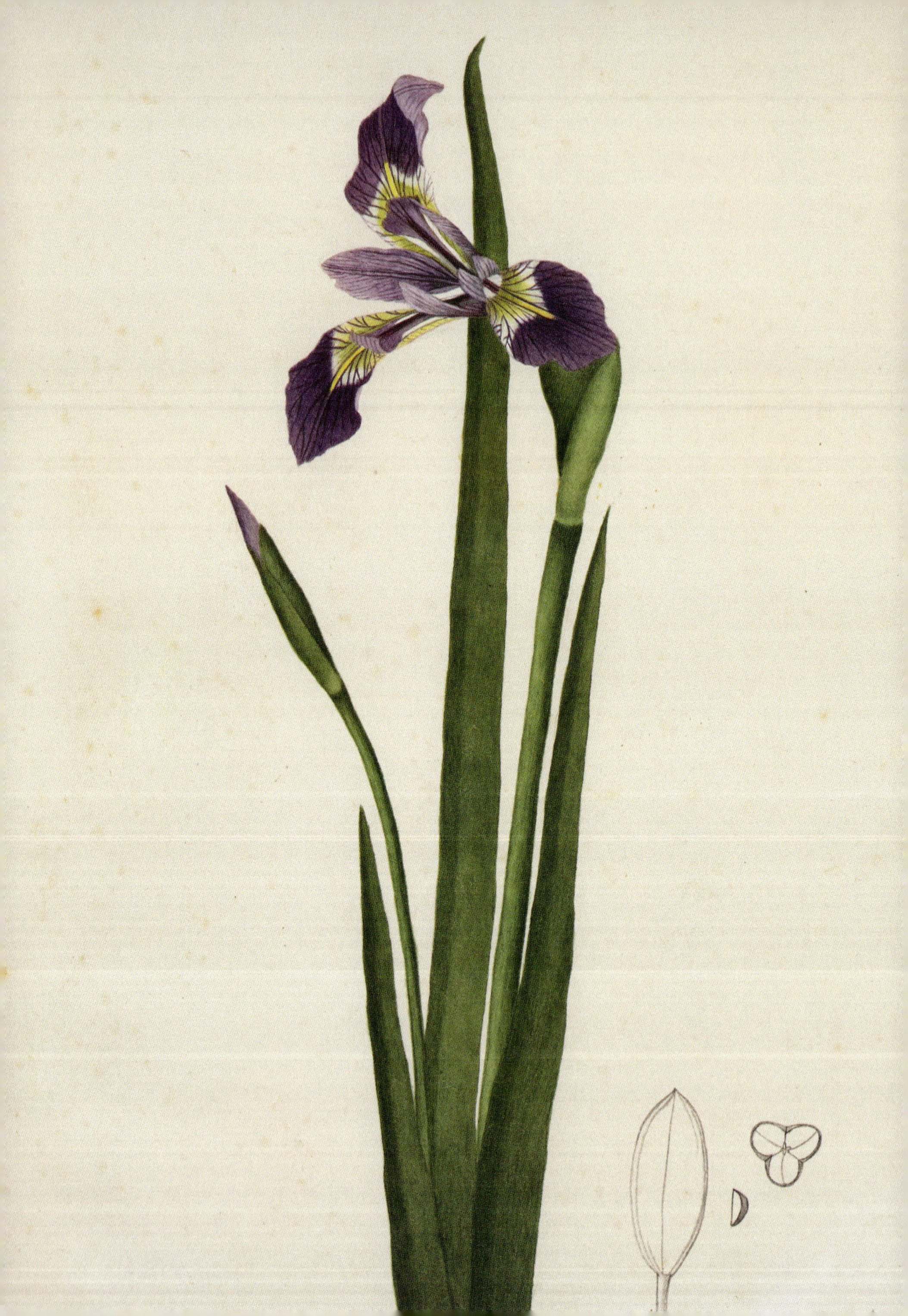

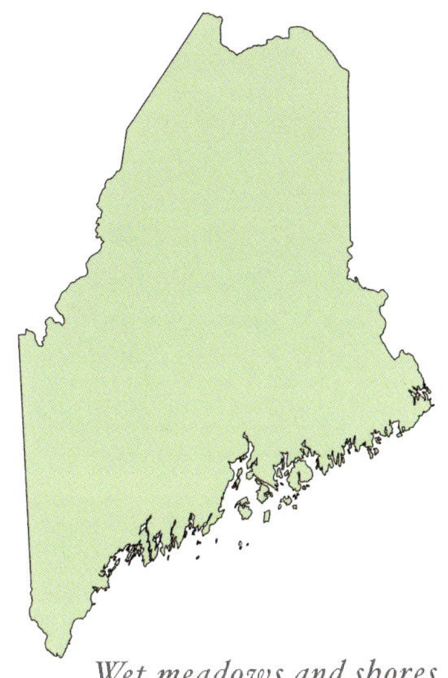

Wet meadows and shores

Furbish Observed At:

Location unknown

BLUE IRIS

Iris versicolor

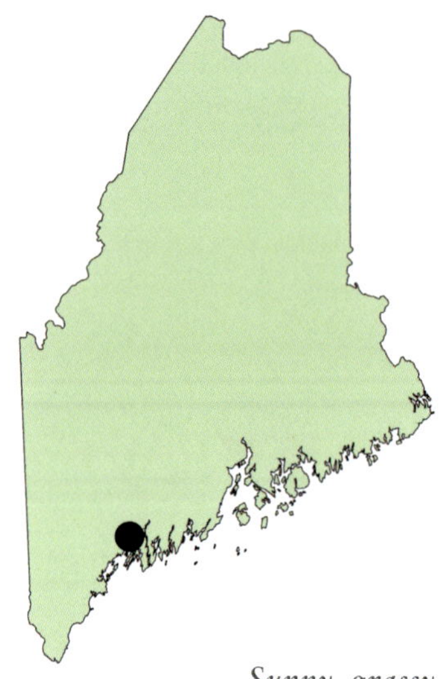

Sunny, grassy slopes and meadows

Furbish Observed At:

Brunswick (1874)

BLACK-EYED SUSAN

Rudbeckia hirta

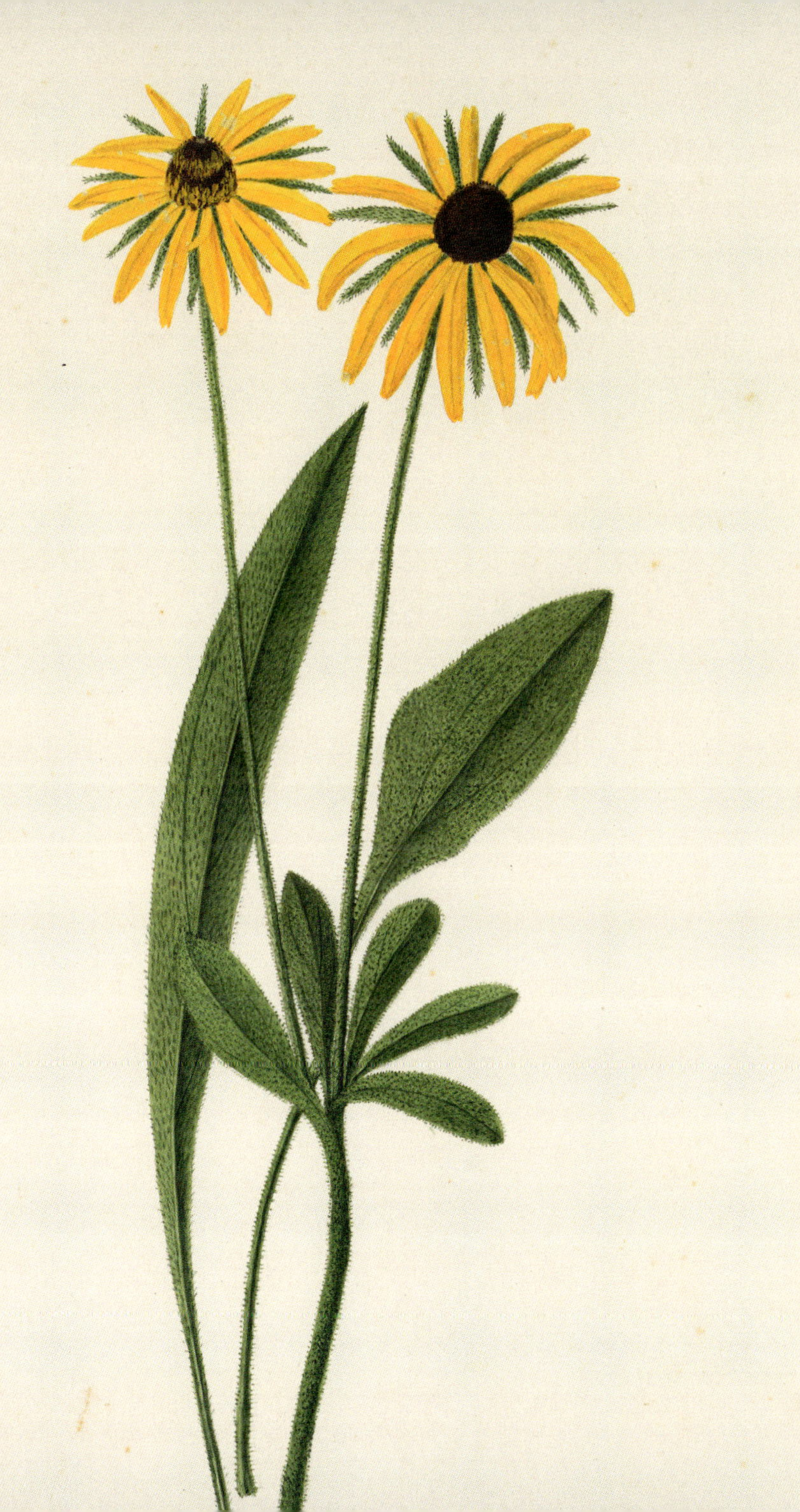

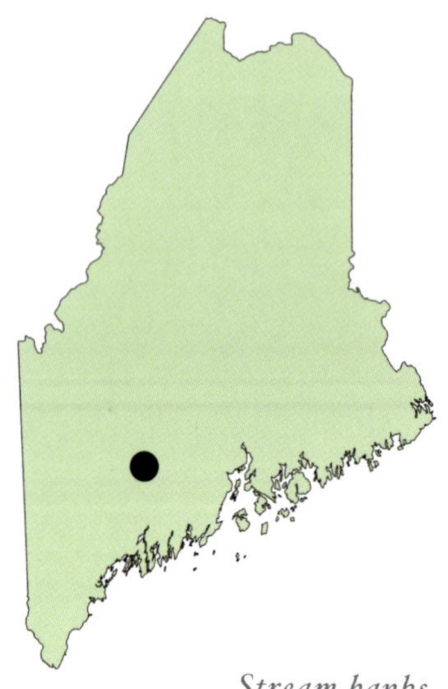

Stream banks, thickets, and ditches

Furbish Observed At:

Fayette (1877)

SCARLET BEE-BALM

Monarda didyma

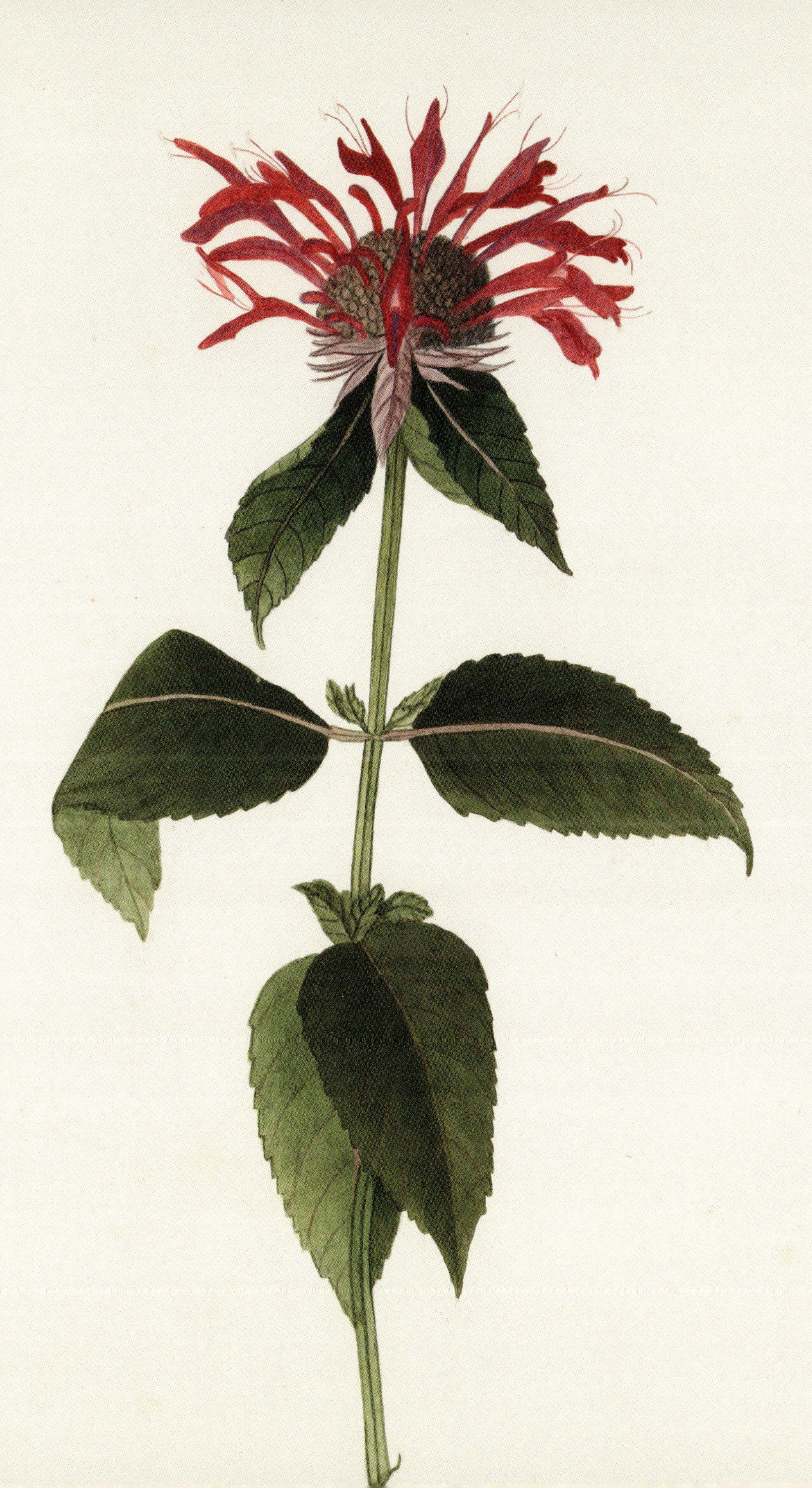

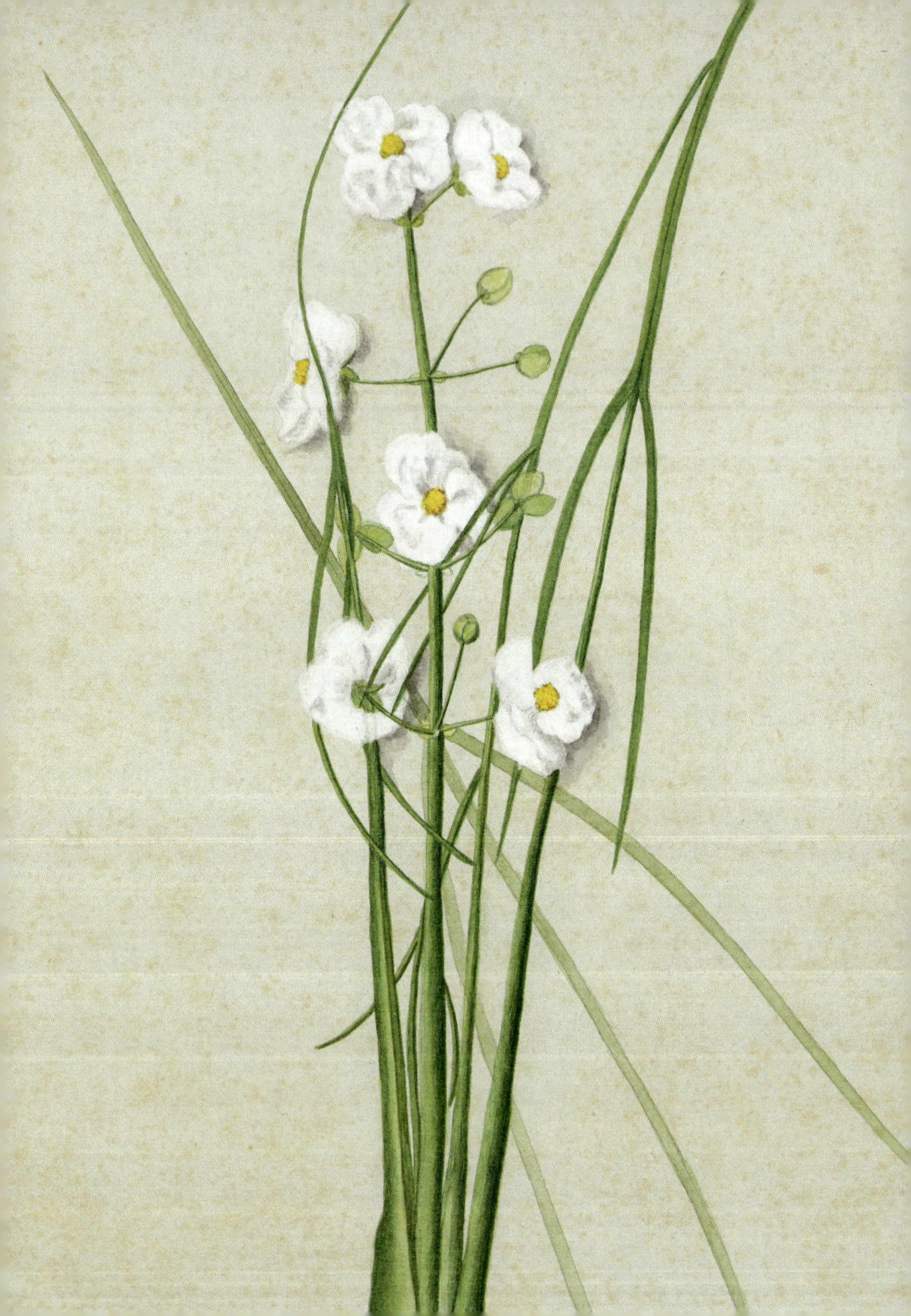

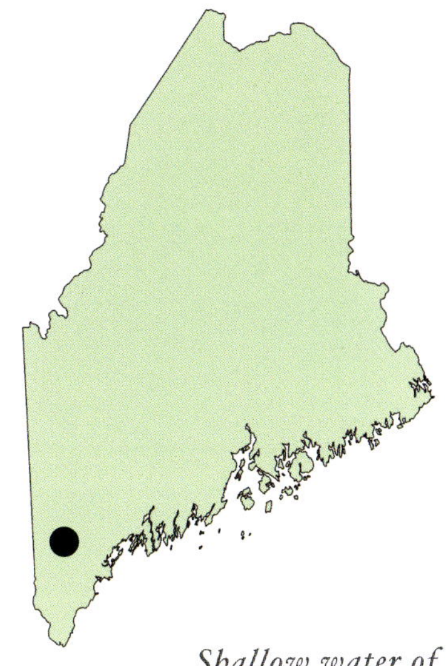

Shallow water of shores and wetlands

Furbish Observed At:

West Baldwin (1900)

COMMON ARROWHEAD

Sagittaria latifolia

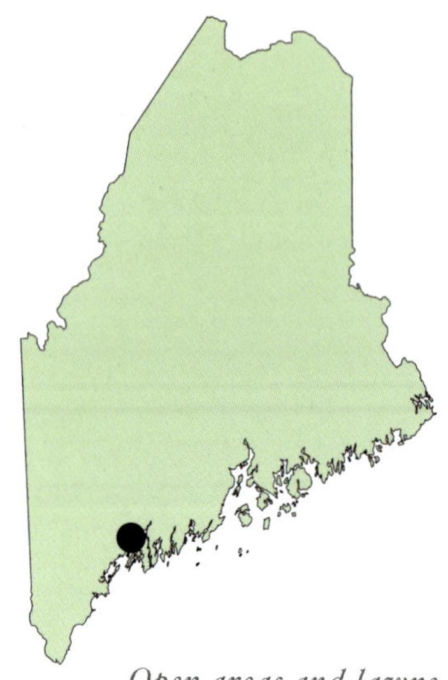

Open areas and lawns

Furbish Observed At:

Brunswick (1870)

COMMON SHEEP SORREL

Rumex acetosella

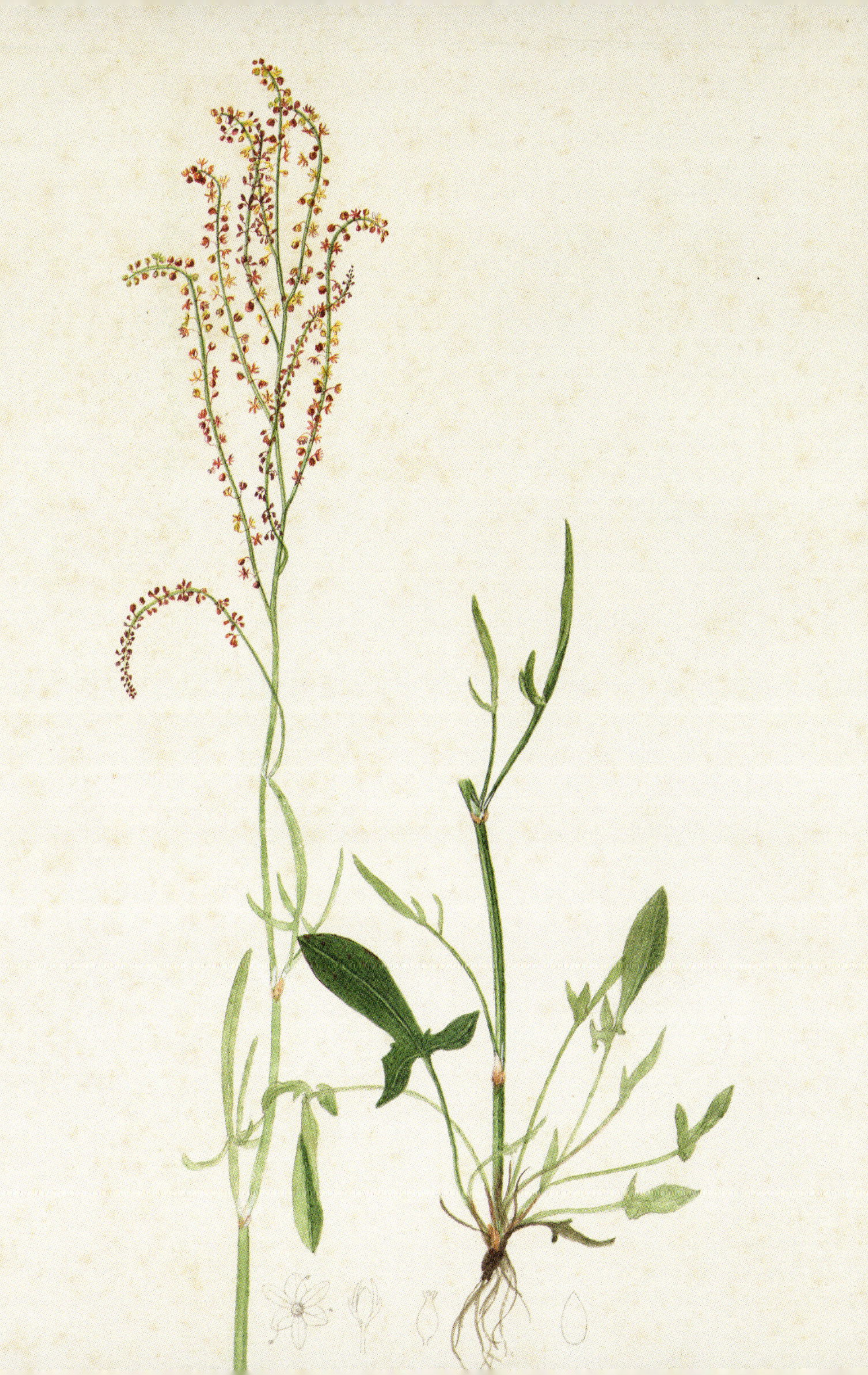

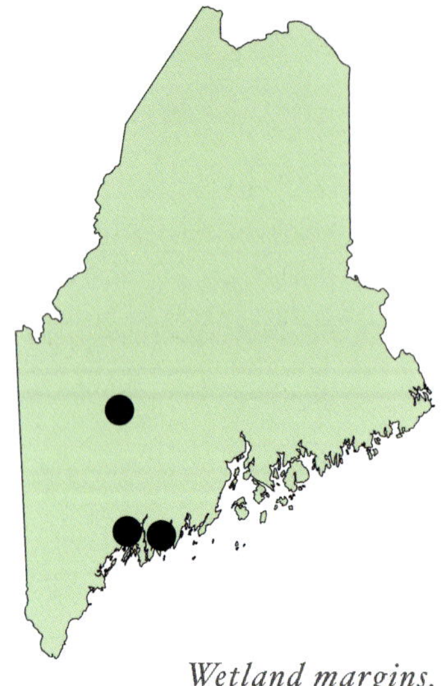

Wetland margins,
forests, and fields

Furbish Observed At:

Brunswick (1870)
Strong (1882)
West Bath (1892)

YELLOW AVENS

Geum allepicum

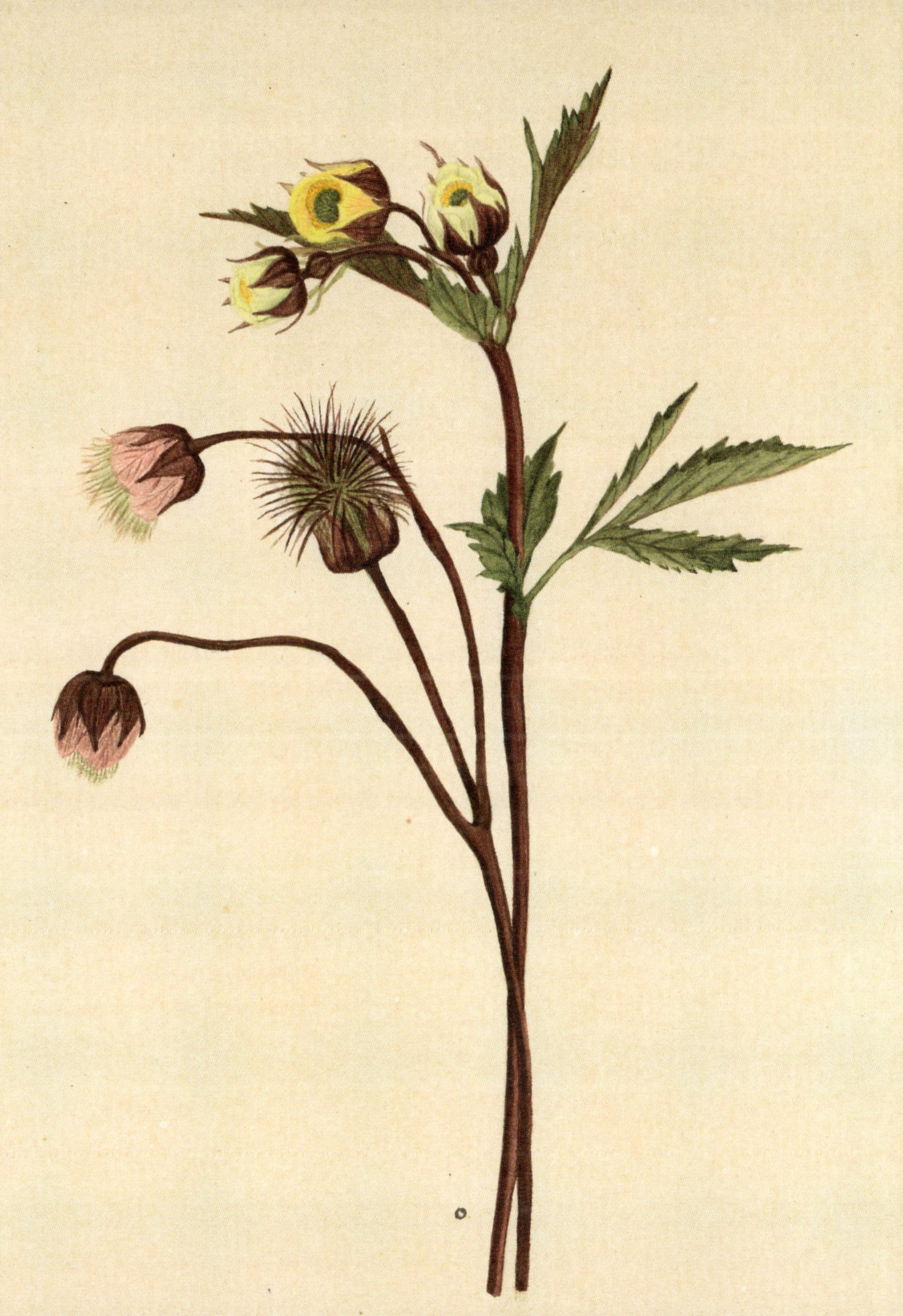

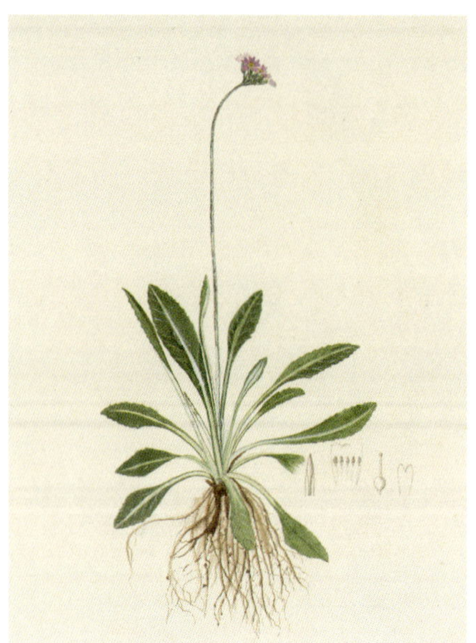

Bird's-eye primrose
(Primula laurentiana)

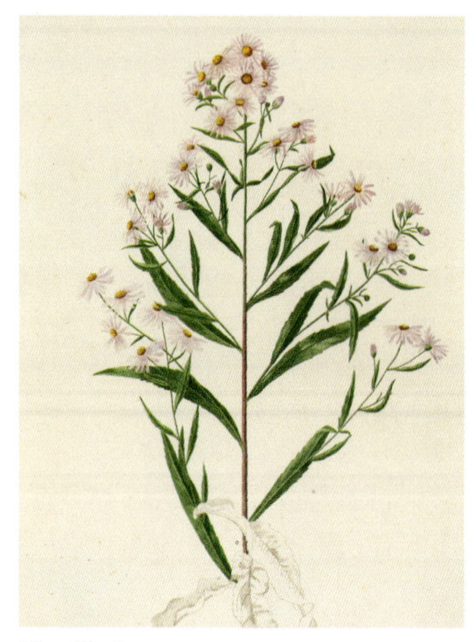

New York aster
(Symphyotrichum novi-belgii)

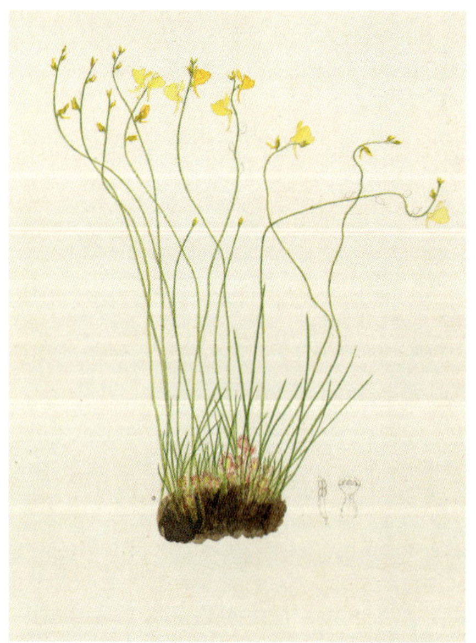

Horned bladderwort
(Utricularia cornuta)

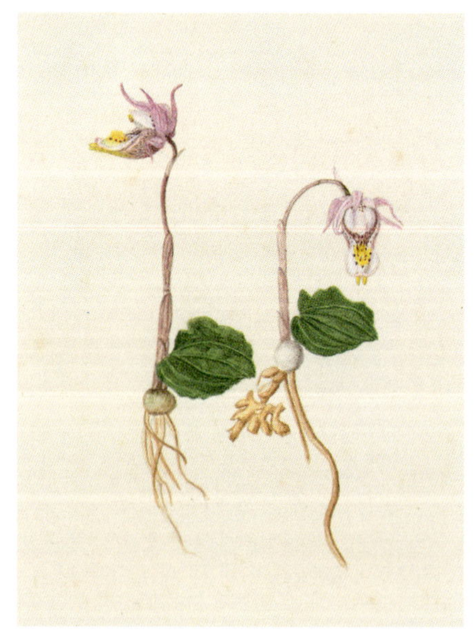

Fairy-slipper
(Calypso bulbosa)

A real testament to [Kate Furbish's] involvement in the botanical community is the numerous times her name appears in the first volume of Rhodora *in association with her diverse collections.*

Kate Furbish and her contemporaries were living in exciting times for botany in New England—interest and engagement in natural history were peaking in the 1890s. This upswelling of general interest and study was foundational for two momentous occasions in 1895, the establishment of both the Josselyn Botanical Society of Maine and the New England Botanical Club, which still enjoy active membership to this day. Furbish and her friend Fernald were among the founding members of the Josselyn Botanical Society. It was Fernald, in fact, who suggested the new society be named after Maine's earliest European botanical explorer, John Josselyn. Both Fernald and Furbish were named as vice presidents in that first year. The society met — and still meets — in a different location around the state each summer, and members through the years have enjoyed several days together with lectures and forays to explore the plants of the particular region. For Furbish and her fellow members, the society provided great social enjoyment and a united focus on furthering knowledge about Maine's wild plants.

The New England Botanical Club, in contrast, was organized

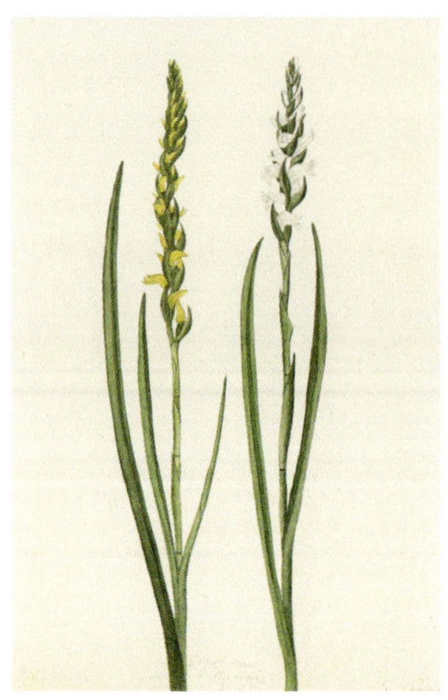

Nodding ladies'-tresses
(Spiranthes cernua)

"for the promotion of social intercourse and the dissemination of local and general information among gentlemen interested in the flora of New England" and as such was open to neither Furbish nor any woman until much later. However, the journal of the New England Botanical Club, *Rhodora,* established in 1899, did not bar contributions by women, and none other than the industrious Kate Furbish was the first woman to contribute to it. She wrote on her collection of a kind of forget-me-not in Maine, which was an earlier collection in New England than had been previously reported. Clearly, while women were not allowed membership in the club until the 1960s, they—and especially Furbish during the club's early years—were contributing to the body of scientific work produced in New England through their discoveries and collections.

Furbish continued to canvass the state in search of plants in the early 1900s, visiting Sebago, Baldwin, Kennebunkport, West Bath, Old Orchard Beach, and Scarborough, as well as her usual haunts such as Brunswick, Wells, Fayette, and Harpswell. She published again in *Rhodora*, reporting on her discovery of the alpine bitter-cress growing in an unusual location and habitat. Her personal herbarium collection was also recognized in *Rhodora* in a survey of New England herbaria.

I can see her as I saw her then a little woman with uplifted head, already turned gray, in animated talk, or with bowed face using her keen eyes along a forest trail, or up a mountain path. She had the sort of eyes that were made for seeing, and nothing escaped the swift circle of her glance. Her feet were as untiring as her eyes, and she could out-last many a younger woman on a cliff-side climb or river-bank scramble.

—"Joss" Louise Coburn, describing her friend, Kate Furbish

In 1902 she made her last long-distance expedition, traveling to the far eastern reaches of Maine in Cutler, Machias, and Lubec. She remained in Washington County from July into September and more than 160 specimens were added to her collection from that trip.

Furbish remained productive in her later years, although she was plagued by neuralgia. As the new century continued on, she became more alone, having lost all her younger brothers and her dear friends Anne Jackson and George Davenport. Still, showing her "tenacity to life-long purpose," she continued her work, collecting and rendering plants from along the coast in Bar Harbor, Phippsburg, Freeport, Isle au Haut, Wells, and as always, Brunswick. Those losses, however, must have made her sense that her work, no matter how dear and vital to her happiness, could not go on forever.

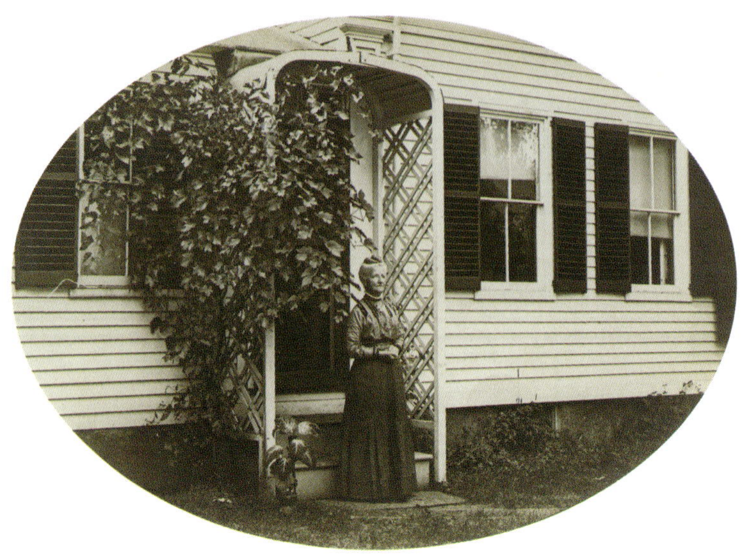

Kate Furbish in front of her Brunswick home c. early 1900s.

Accordingly, she called upon her young friend Fernald, of whom she had become increasingly fond. She sought his advice about setting her botanical collections in order, and in 1908, when she was seventy-four, he came to her aid, spending several days at her Brunswick home helping to sort and organize her collection of more than 8,000 sheets. The vast majority of her specimens went to the New England Botanical Club, where her labels read: "Herbarium of Kate Furbish, Received November, 1908." Some have wondered why she, who was so devoted to Maine and its flora, sent her specimens out of state. The answer likely lies in her ties to Fernald, whom she had known most of his life, and to whom she had already been sending specimens for nearly two decades.

Her masterwork, however, her great collection of watercolor botanical illustrations, which had consumed half of her life, would

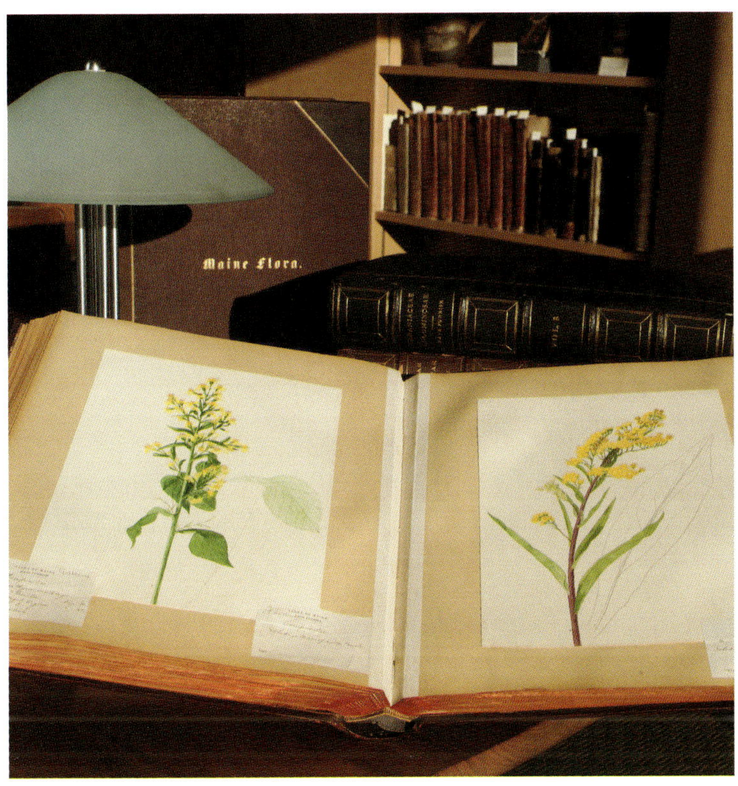

One of fourteen volumes of illustrations of Maine plants and flowers Furbish bequeathed to Bowdoin College.

stay in Maine. Setting all her botanical affairs in order, she gifted the collection to Bowdoin College in hopes that the 1,326 sheets within would instruct the young and future botanists of Maine. With help from Fernald, she assembled the results of her years of labor into sixteen large volumes, organized according to the taxonomy of her day, and presented them to the college late in the same year as she donated her herbarium specimens to the New England Botanical Club.

Having found safe harbor for her collections and paintings at institutions where they would be used and appreciated, she continued on in the pursuit of botany. She remained active in the Josselyn Botanical Society and in the summer of 1909 she continued her collecting. The following year, she made an extensive collection from Monhegan Island and through 1915 she collected hundreds more specimens from mid-coast Maine. At the age of eighty-one, her collecting finally began to slow. Even so, her love for her work never ebbed, and she made a few additional collections well into her eighties, with the last in 1921, when she was eighty-seven.

Kate Furbish passed away on December 6, 1931, at age ninety-seven, and her remains were interred at the Pine Grove Cemetery in Brunswick. Yet her work remained impactful. She became posthumously celebrated,

---

She celebrated her ninetieth birthday in May, 1924. When I called on her not many weeks ago her hair was snow-white but her interest in Botany seemed to be as lively as ever, and her room was littered with dried plants. She told me she could walk by herself over the farm where she was staying, in search of her specimens, and turning the leaves of Gray's Manual to verify a description she read the fine print without glasses.

—"Joss" Louise Coburn, describing her friend, Kate Furbish

---

even outside of botanical circles, when Furbish's lousewort was rediscovered by Dr. Charles Richards of the University of Maine during surveys to complete an environmental impact statement for the proposed Dickey-Lincoln Dam in 1976. The dam threatened to flood 88,000 acres of wilderness around the St. John River, including habitat of the Furbish's lousewort. Because of the endemic nature and extreme rarity of this species, a proposal to list Furbish's lousewort as a federally endangered species was drafted, effectively stalling and ultimately contributing to preventing the dam's construction. Furbish became an environmental heroine and the plant she discovered an icon for the cause to derail the dam's construction.

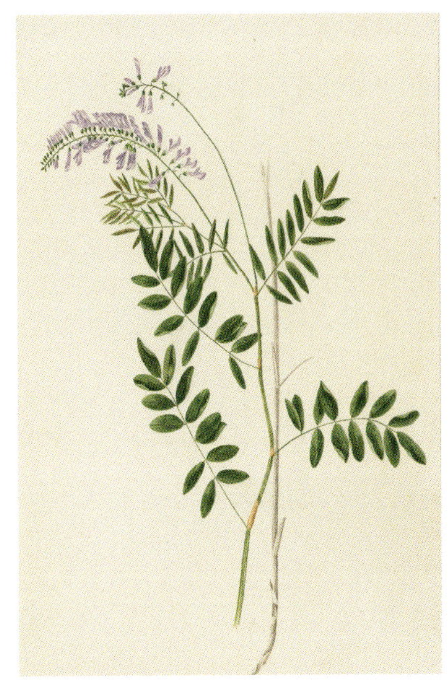

Alpine sweet vetch
(Hedysarum alpinum)

Today, she is remembered and revered both as a dedicated and respected botanist, and as a botanical illustrator. She was a woman both of her time and ahead of her time, leading the way for other women in botany. She collected plants from all sixteen Maine counties, over ninety municipalities and several more unorganized territories. Her specimens, comprising some 8,000 sheets, continue to be used and studied. Two plant taxa, which she discovered in Maine's wild places, were named in her honor. Her collection of paintings is a true treasure of Maine's botanical heritage.

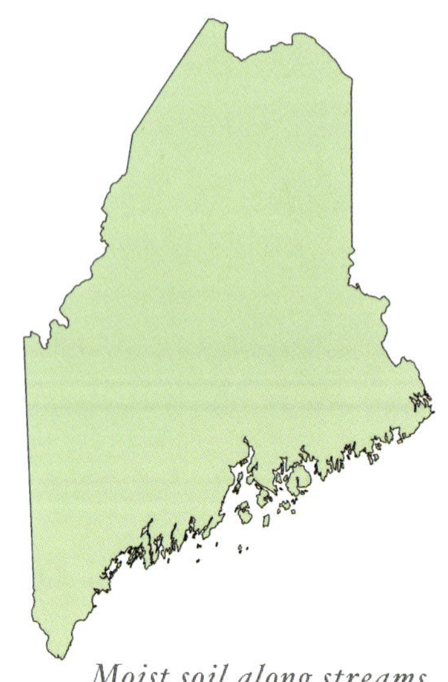

Moist soil along streams, roadsides, beaches, and disturbed areas

Furbish Observed At:

Location unknown

HEDGE FALSE BINDWEED

Calystegia sepium

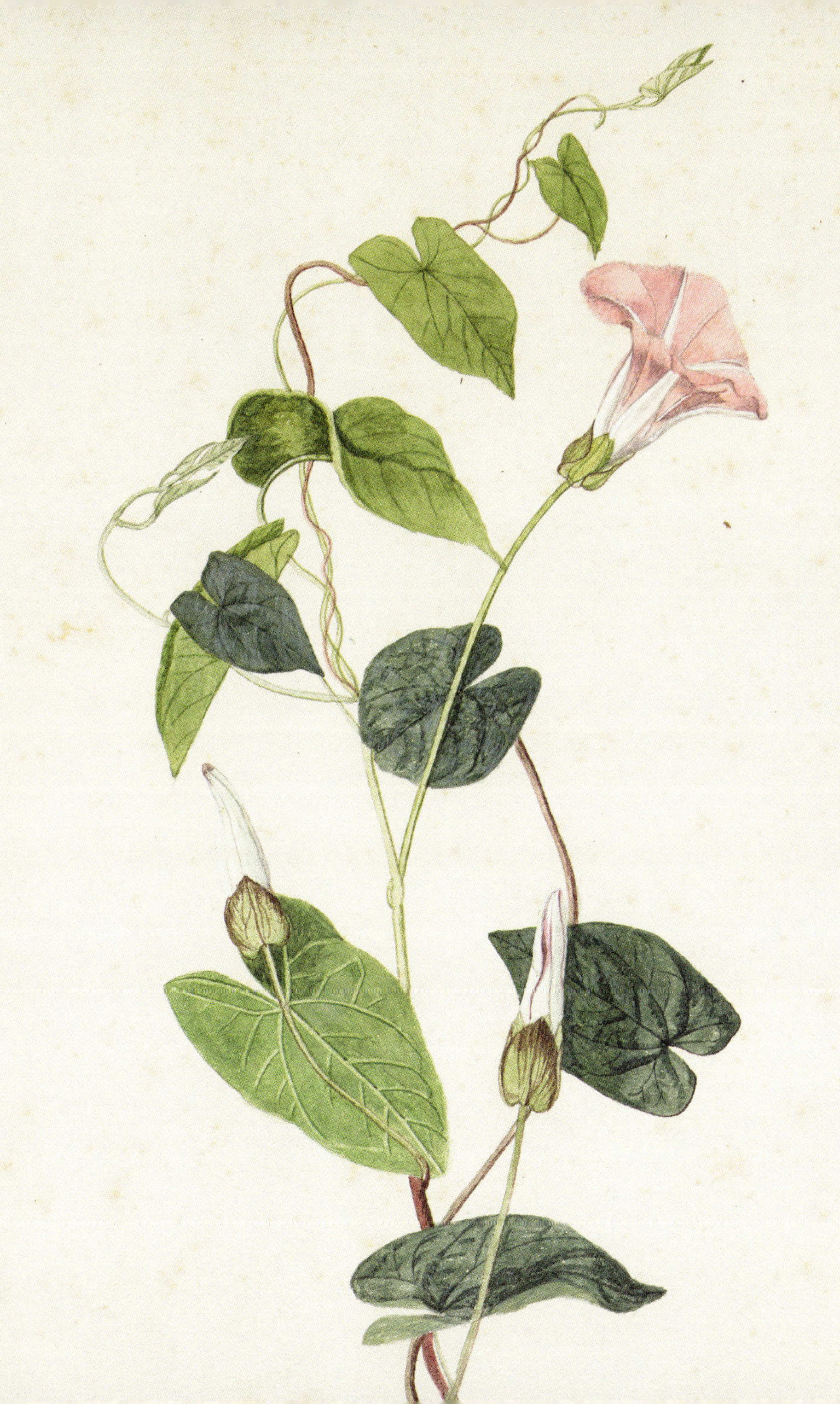

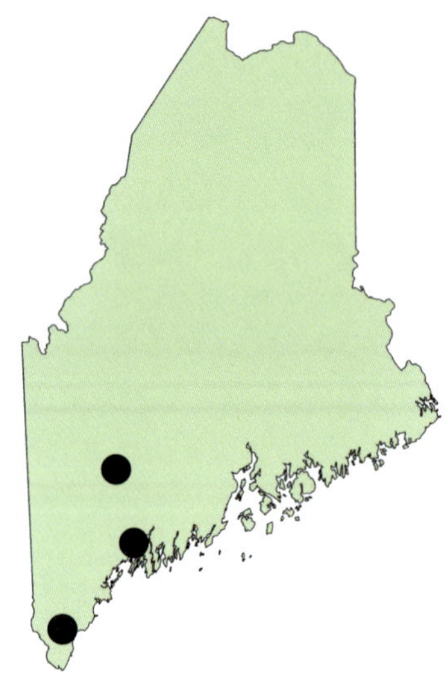

Sandy soil in open sunny areas

Furbish Observed At:

Brunswick (1871)
Wells (1898)
East Livermore (1898)

COMMON MILKWEED

Asclepias syriaca

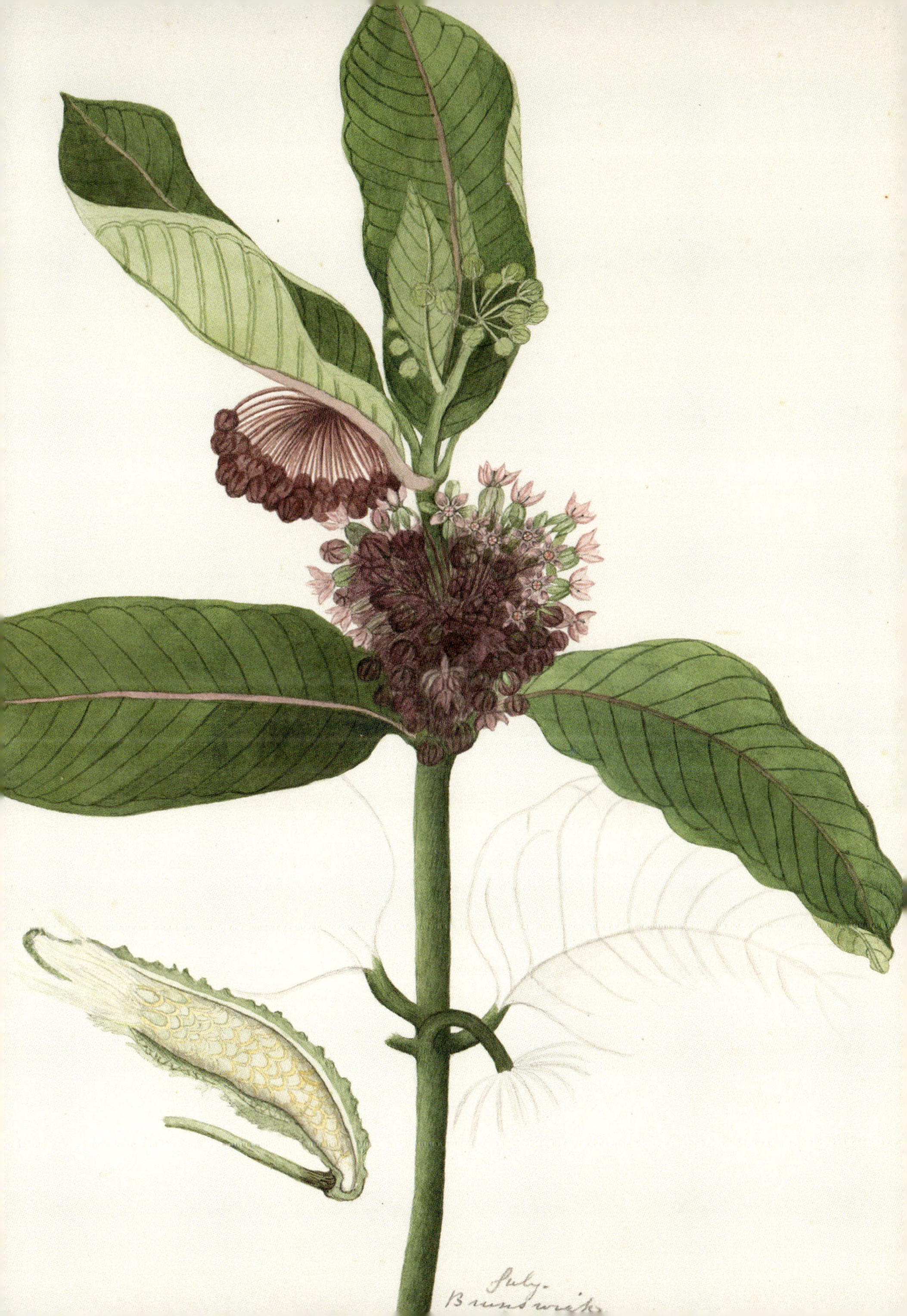
July.
Brunswick

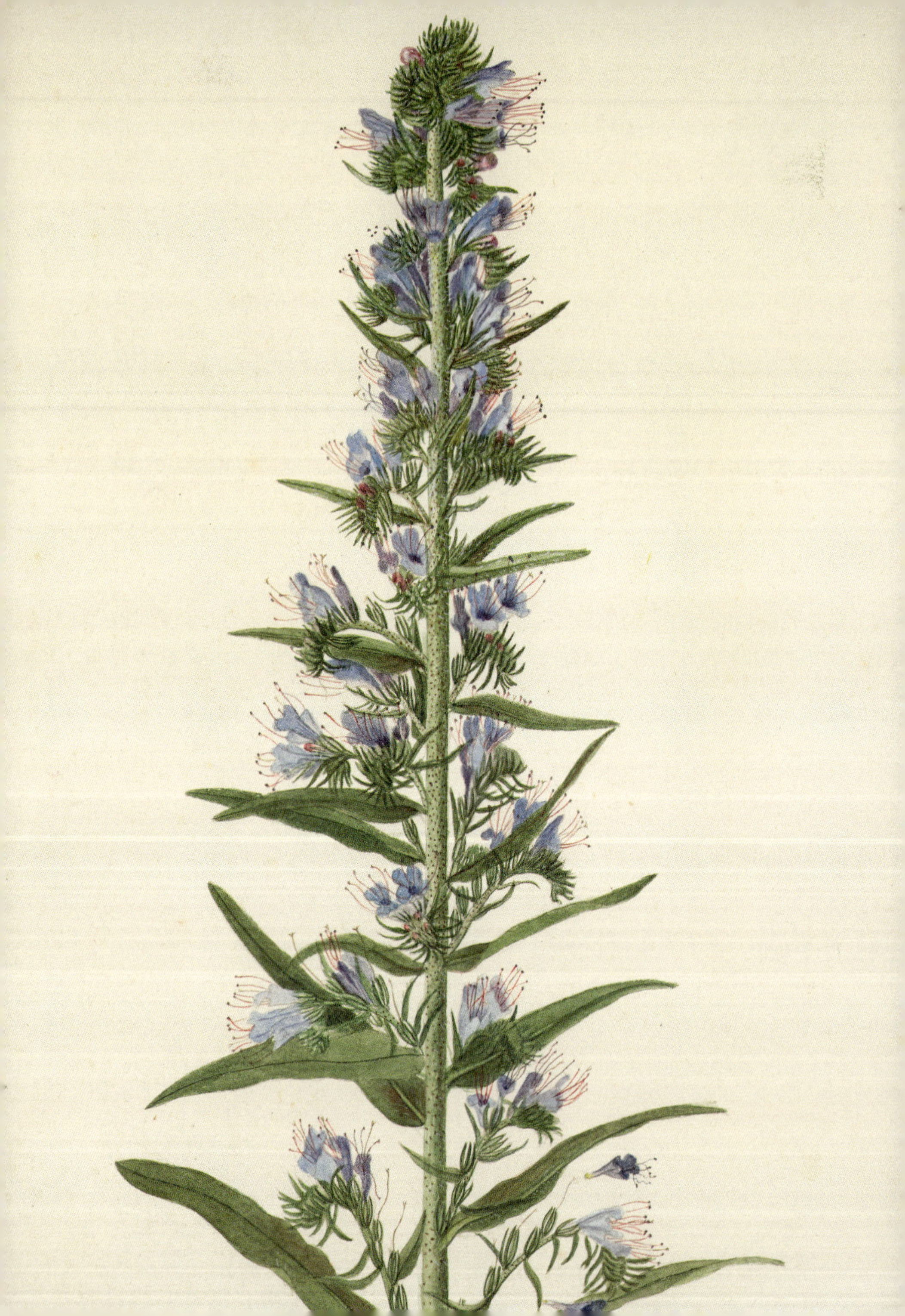

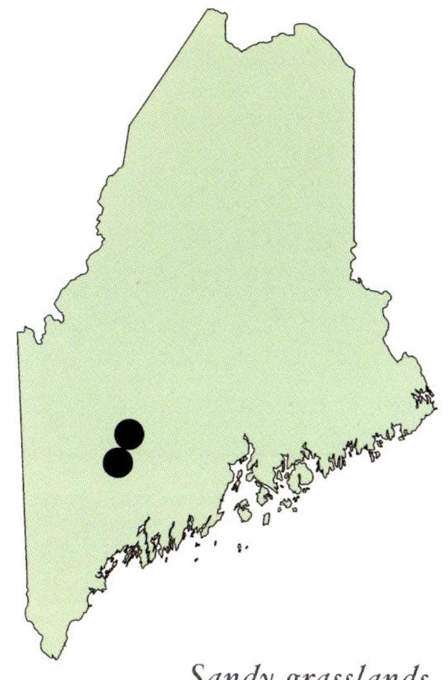

Sandy grasslands, roadsides, and meadows

Furbish Observed At:

Farmington (1888)
East Livermore (1891)

COMMON VIPER'S-BUGLOSS

Echium vulgare

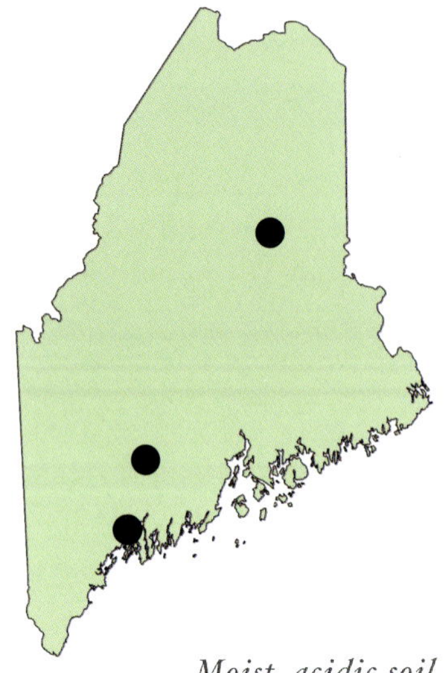

Moist, acidic soil

Furbish Observed At:

Brunswick (1878)
Fayette (1878)
Patten (1881)

PINK LADY'S-SLIPPER

Cypripedium acaule

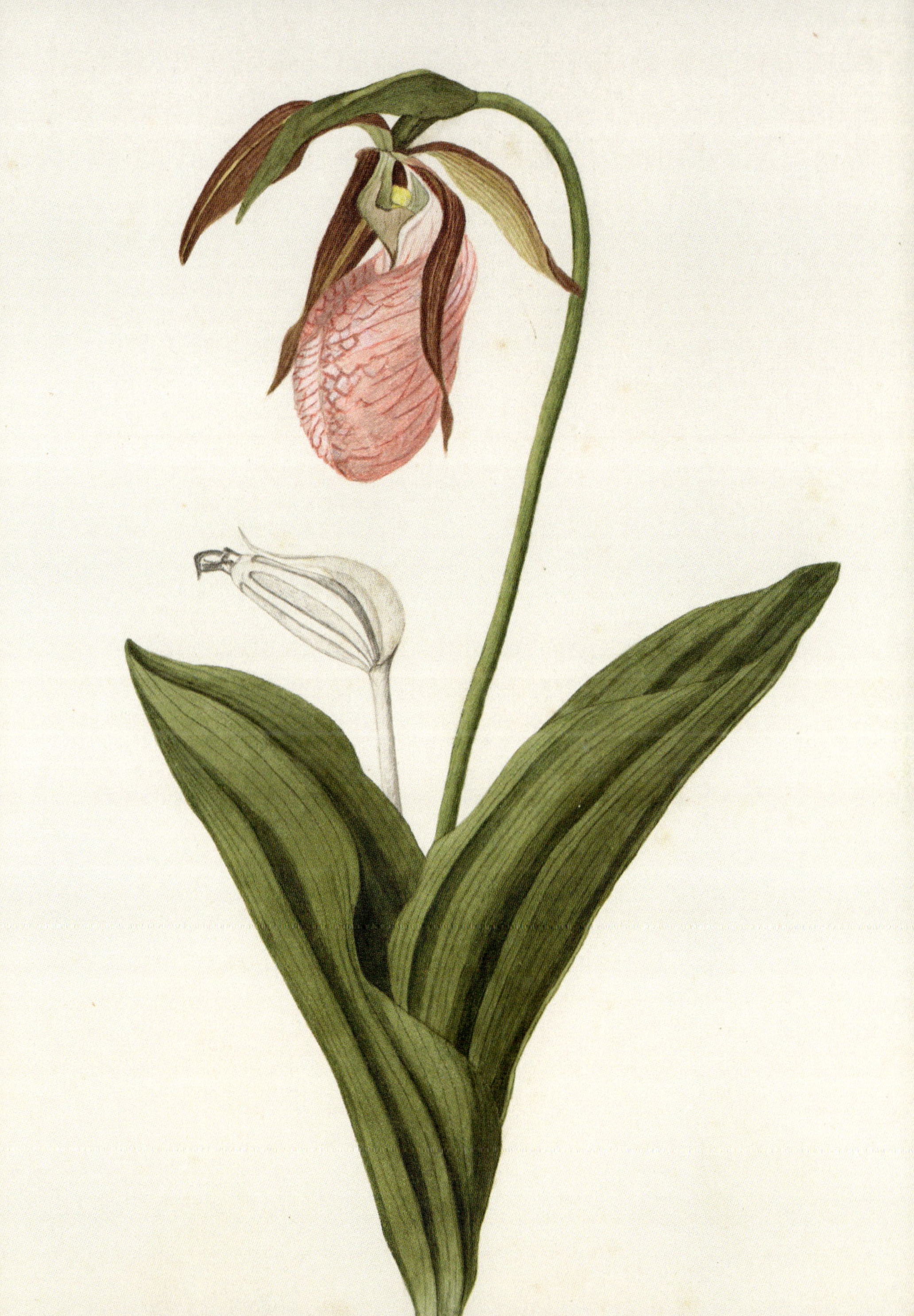

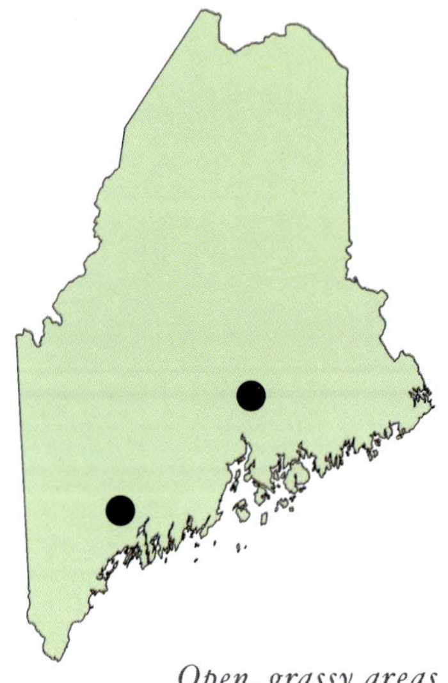

Open, grassy areas and disturbed sites

Furbish Observed At:

Orono (1891)
Lisbon Falls (1906)

BIRD'S-EYE SPEEDWELL

Veronica persica

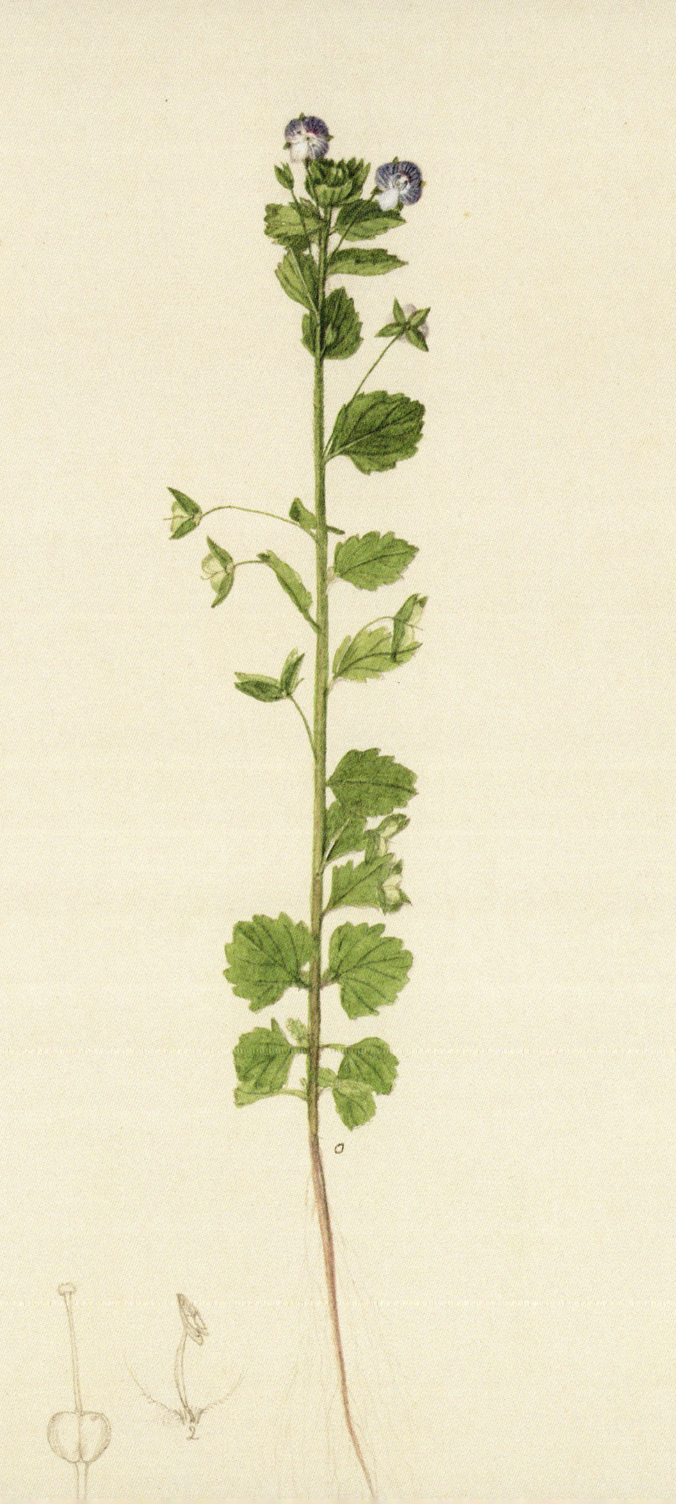

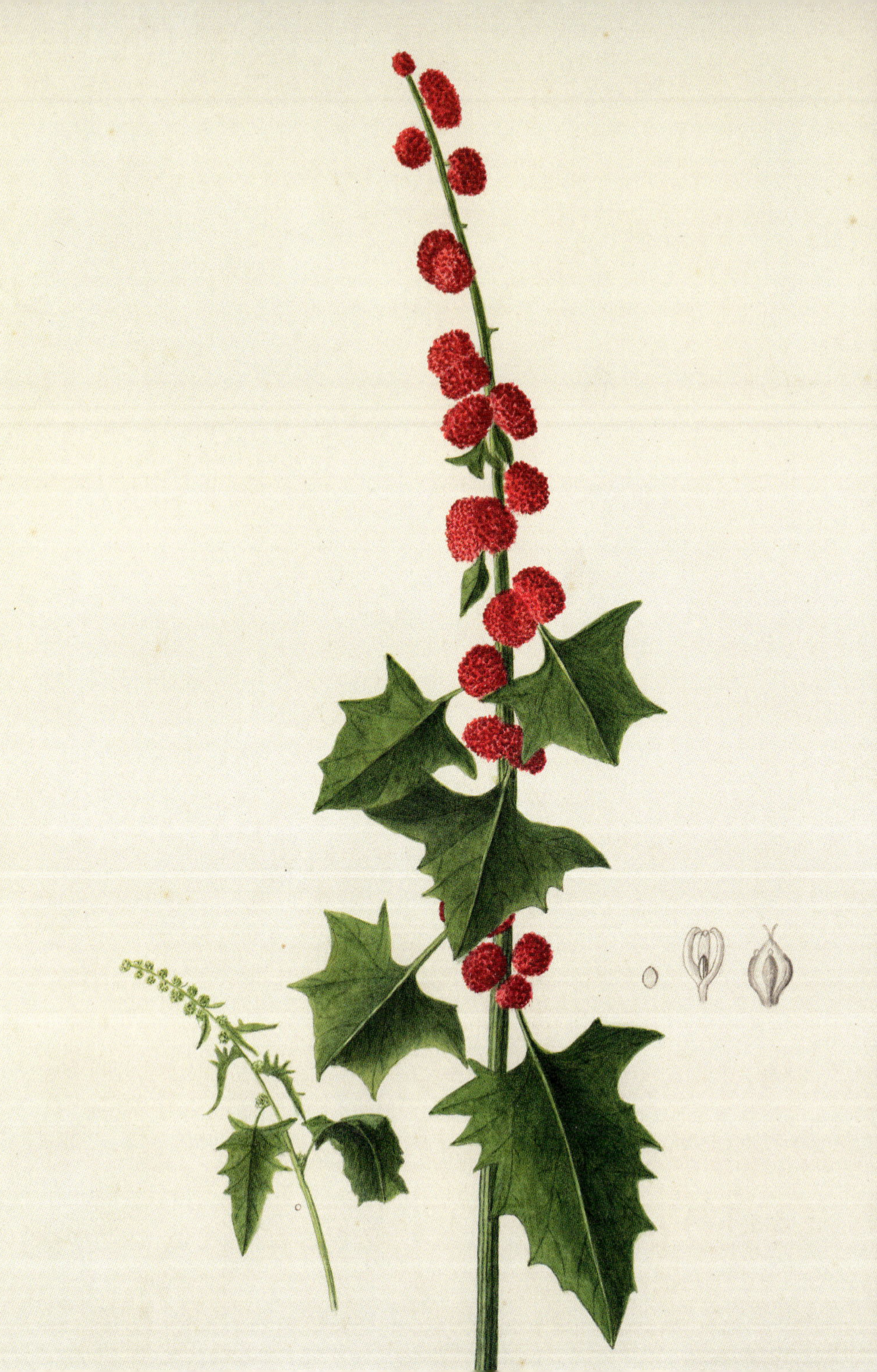

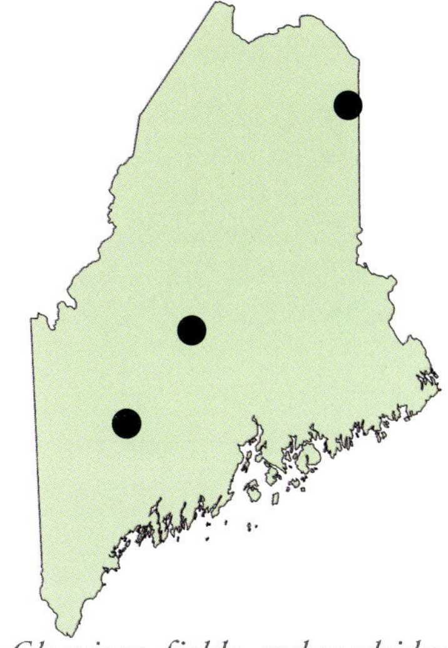

Clearings, fields, and roadsides

Furbish Observed At:

Fort Fairfield (1880)
Kingsbury Plantation (1880)
Chesterville (1898)

STRAWBERRY-BLITE

Chenopodium capitatum

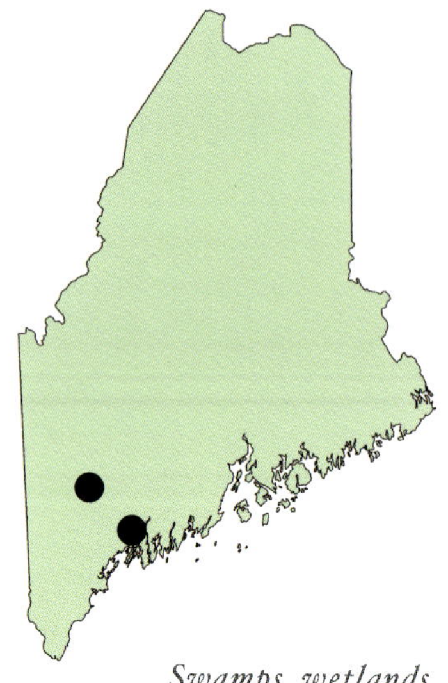

Swamps, wetlands, and shorefronts

Furbish Observed At:

Brunswick (1871)
South Poland (1893)

WHITE TURTLEHEAD

Chelone glabra

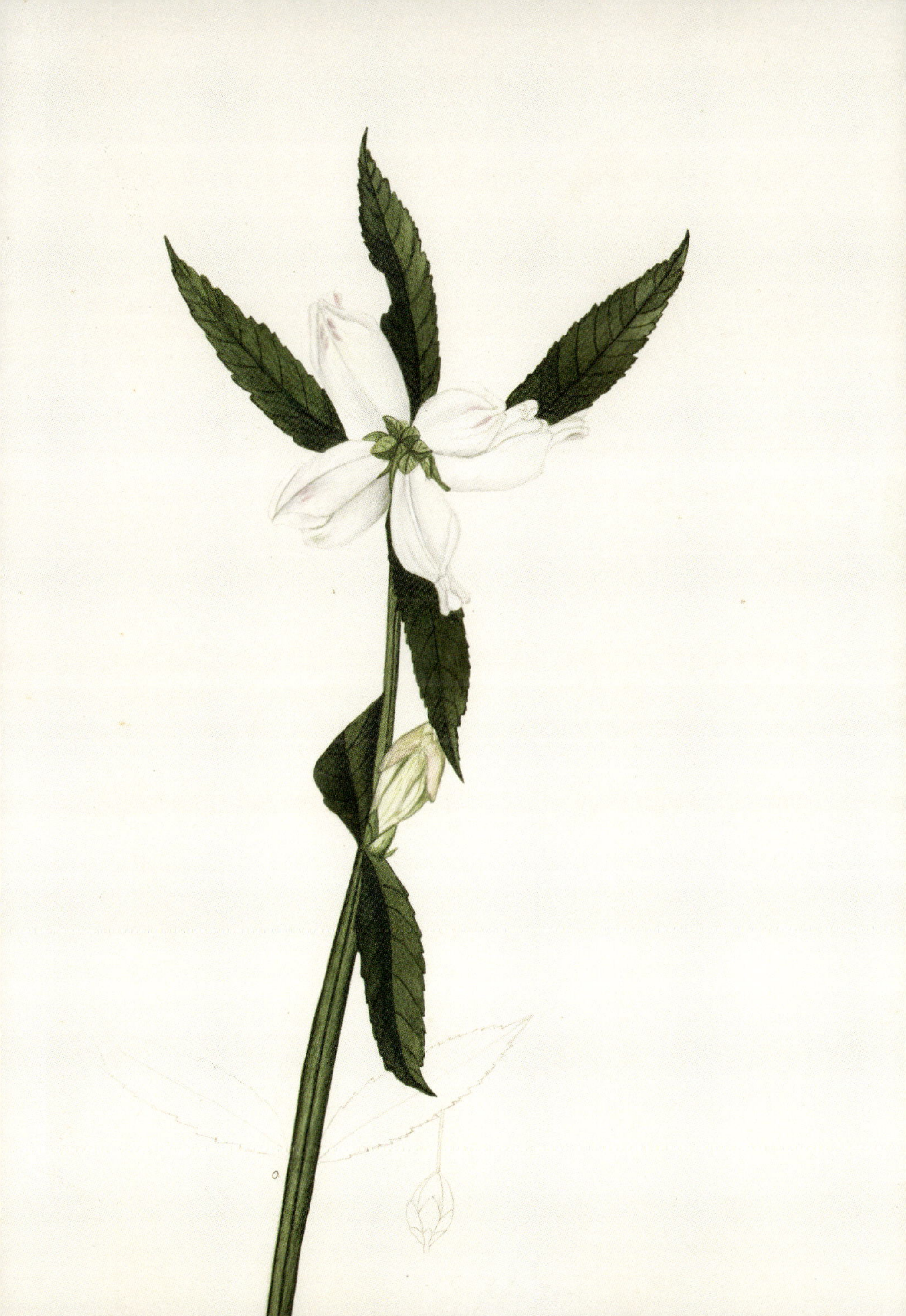

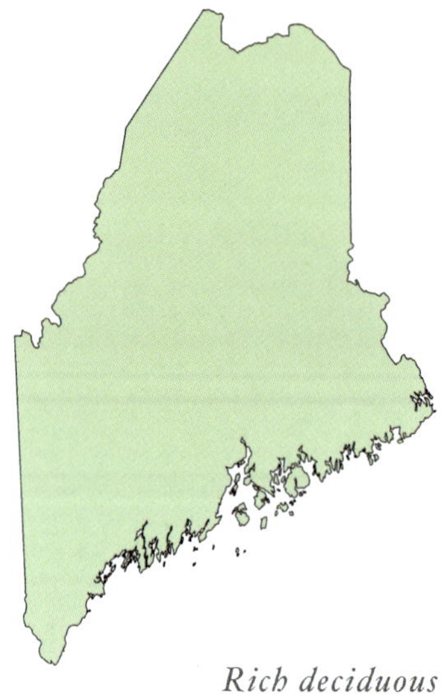

Rich deciduous forests and slopes

Furbish Observed At:

Location unknown

RED WAKEROBIN

Trillium erectum

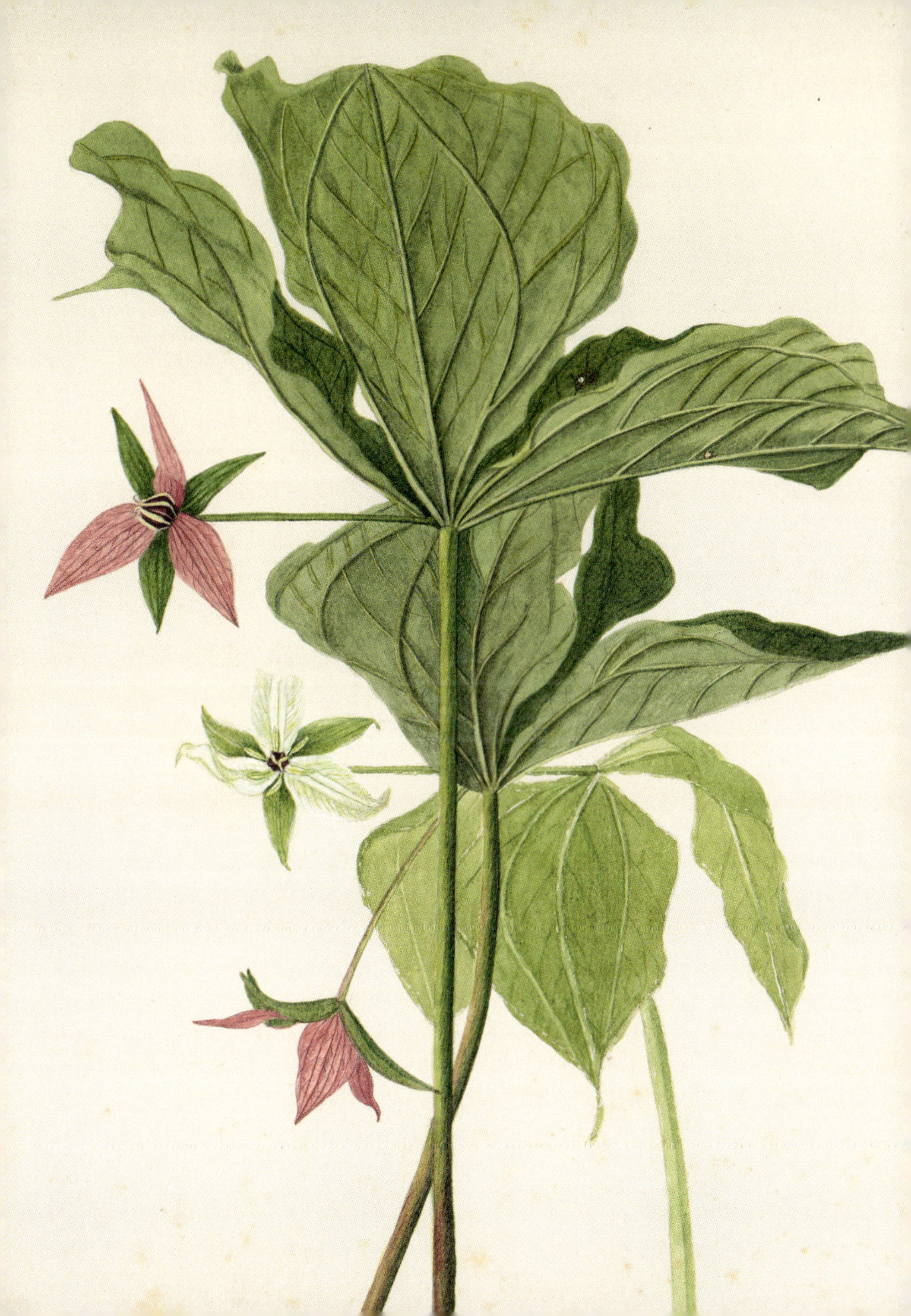

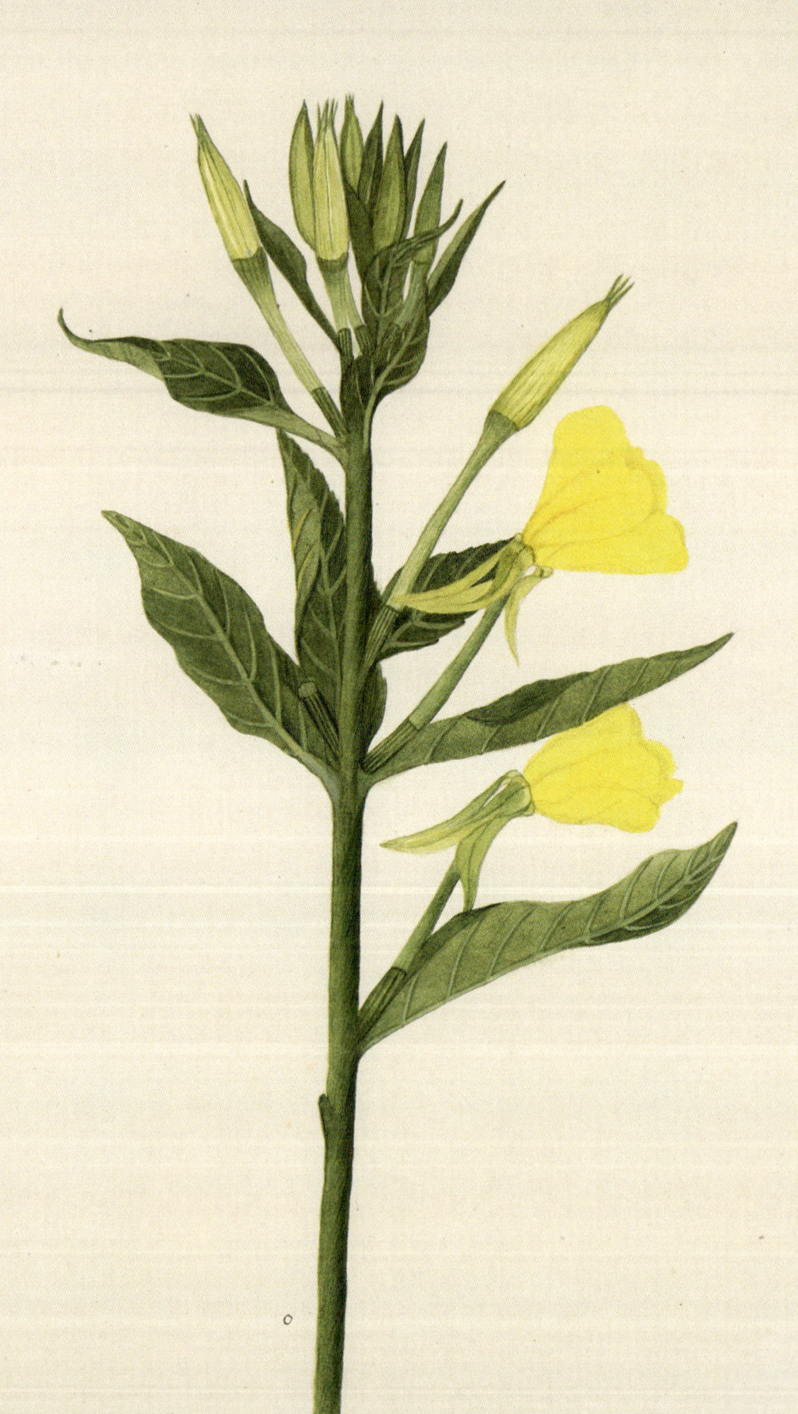

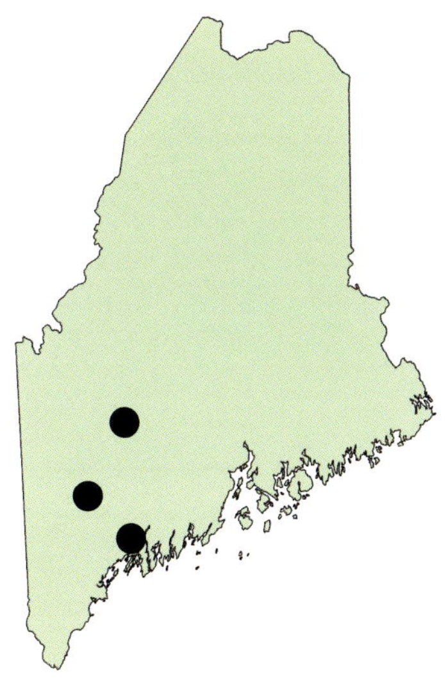

Open fields, roadsides, and other sunny fairly dry areas

Furbish Observed At:

Brunswick (1870)
South Poland (1893)
Farmington (n.d.)

COMMON EVENING PRIMROSE

Oenothera biennis

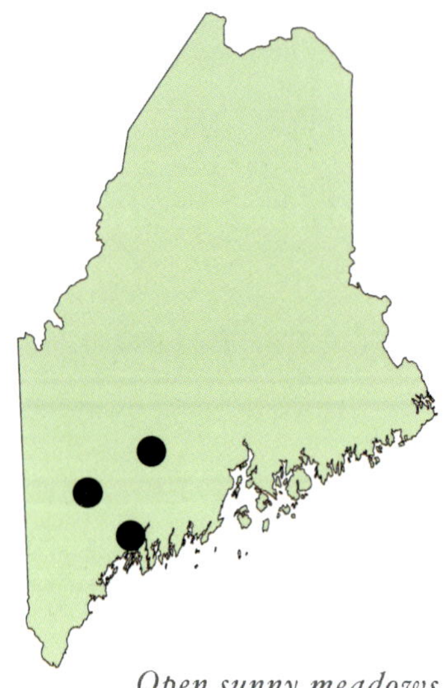

Open sunny meadows and fields and recently disturbed areas

Furbish Observed At:

Brunswick (1877)
South Poland (1893)
Fayette (n.d.)

ROBIN'S PLANTAIN FLEABANE

Erigeron pulchellus

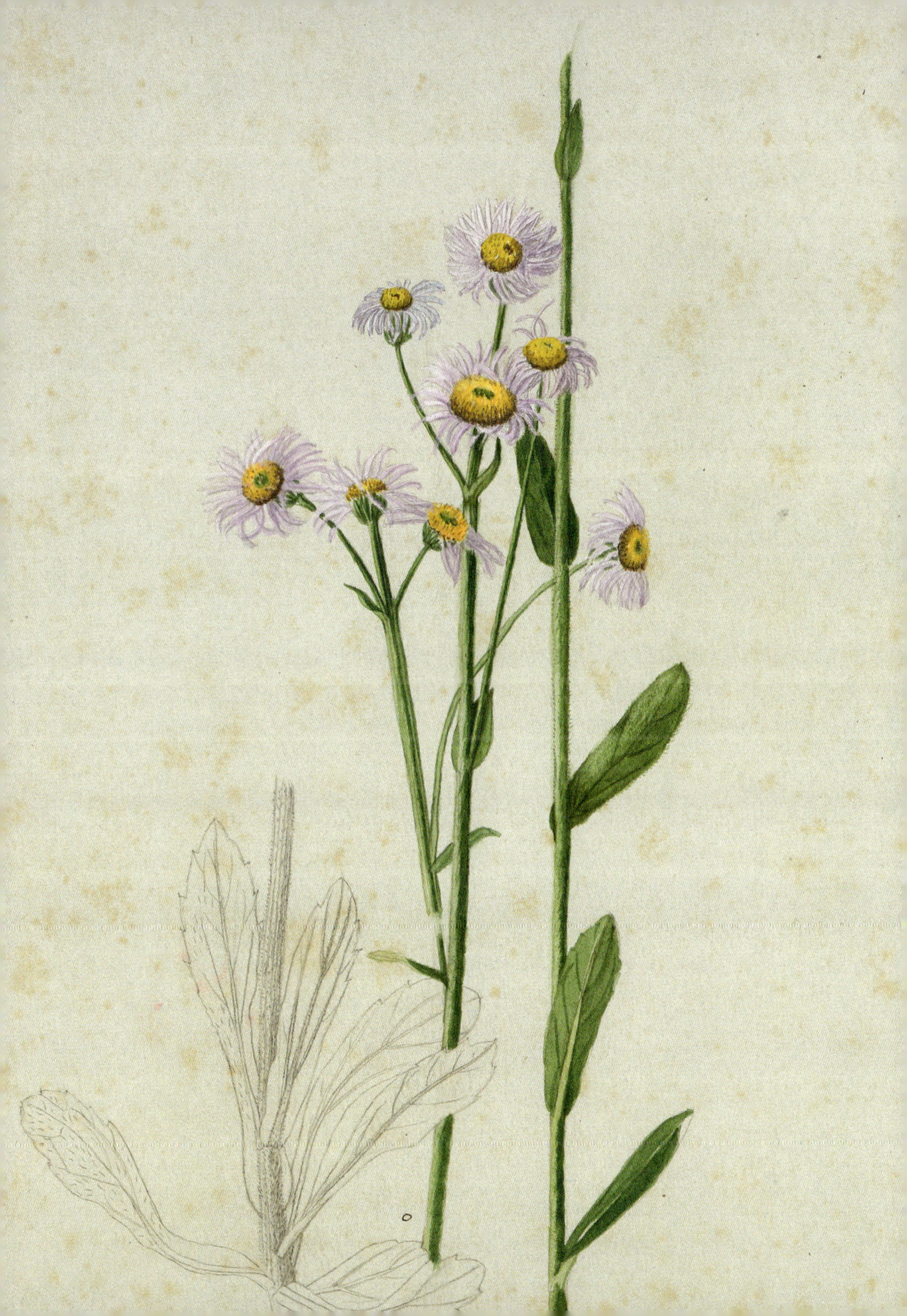

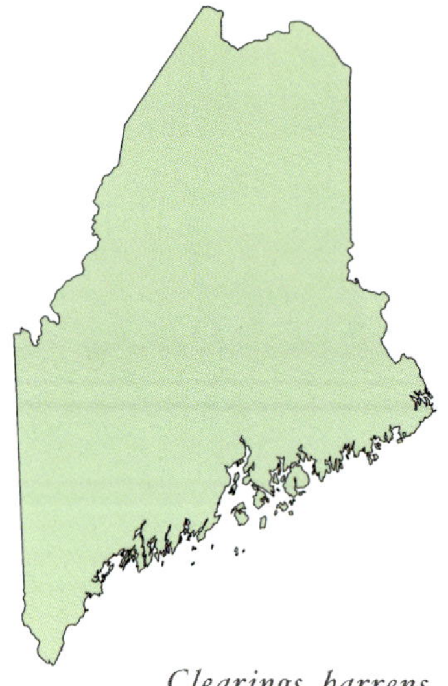

Clearings, barrens, open woodlands

Furbish Observed At:

Location unknown

WOOD LILY

Lilium philadelphicum

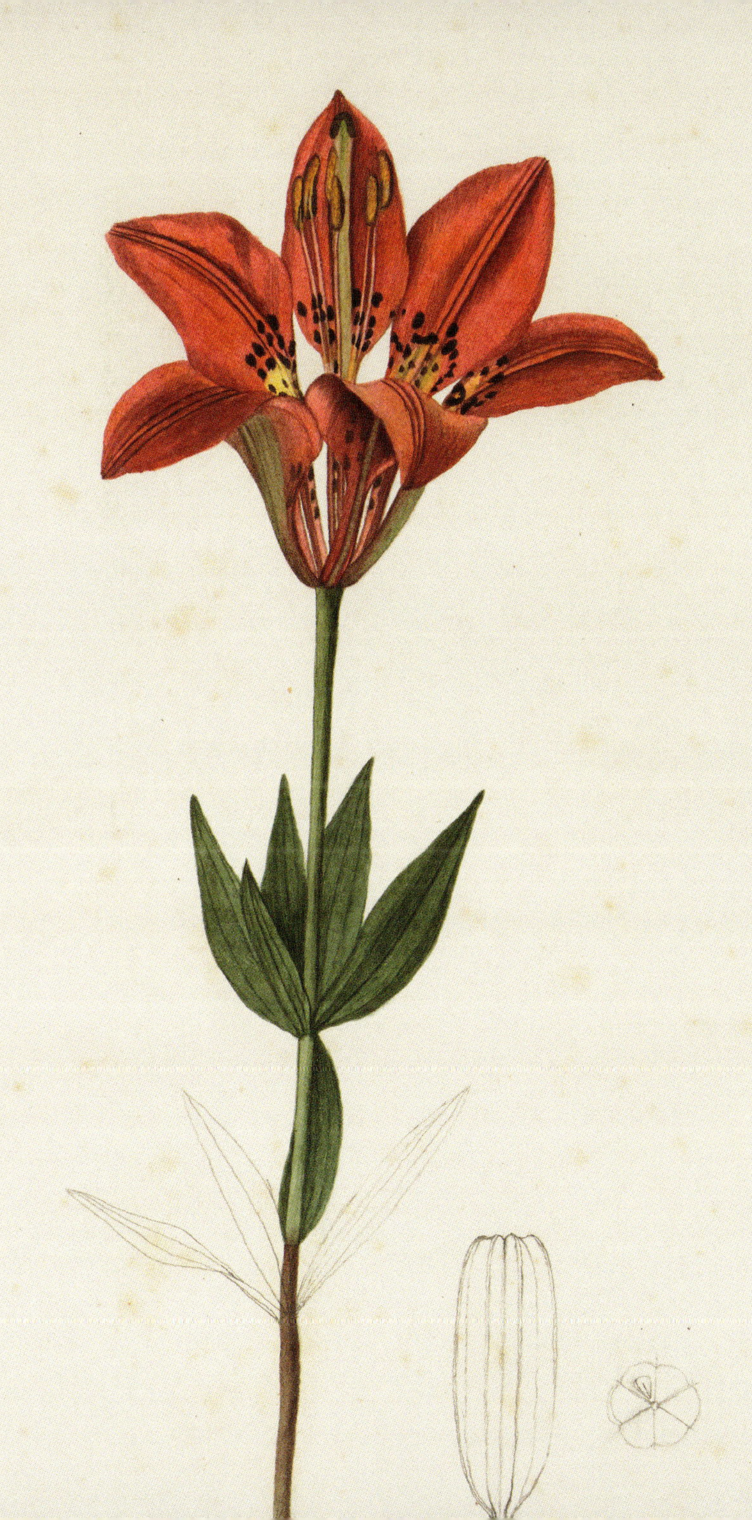

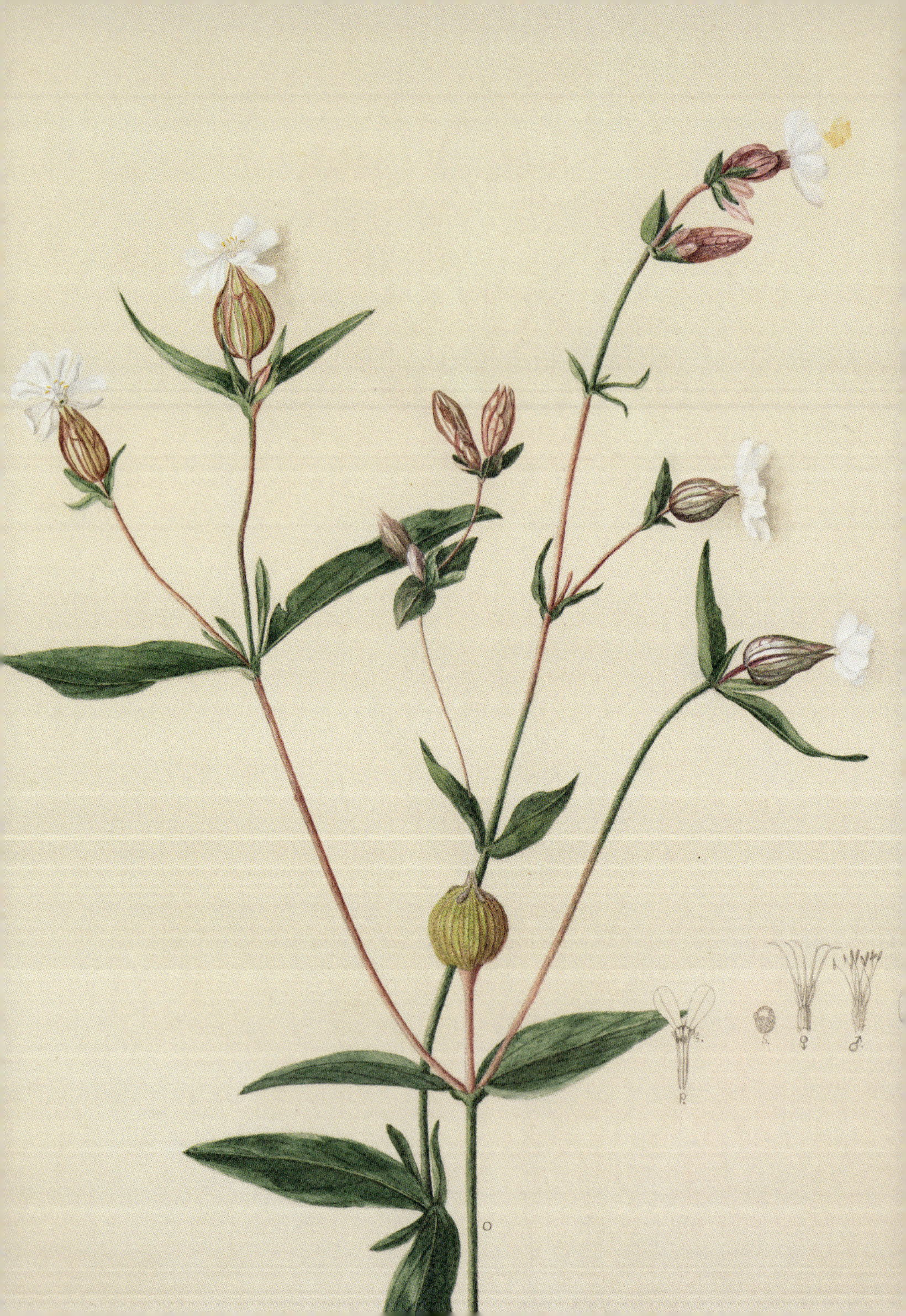

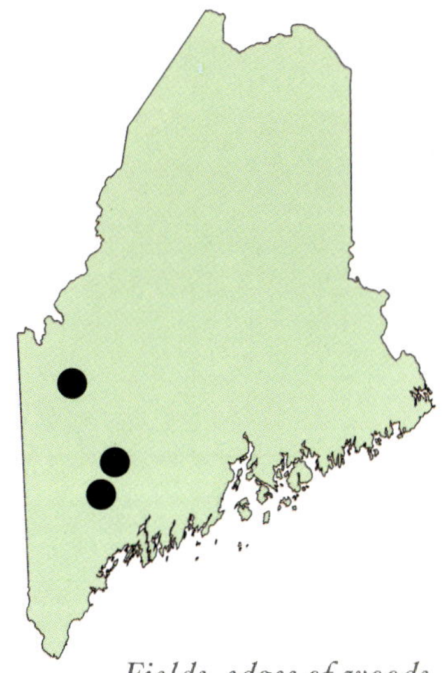

Fields, edges of woods, disturbed areas

Furbish Observed At:

Rangeley (1894)
Sabattus (1901)
East Livermore (1901)

WHITE CAMPION

Silene latifolia

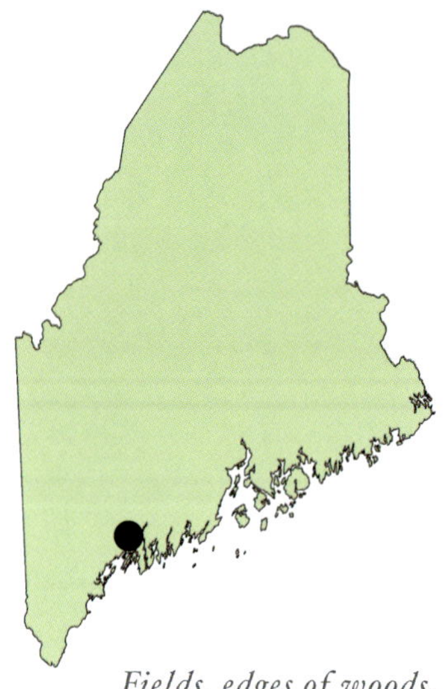

Fields, edges of woods,
disturbed areas,
occasional wetlands

Brunswick (1901)

COMMON VIOLET

Viola sororia

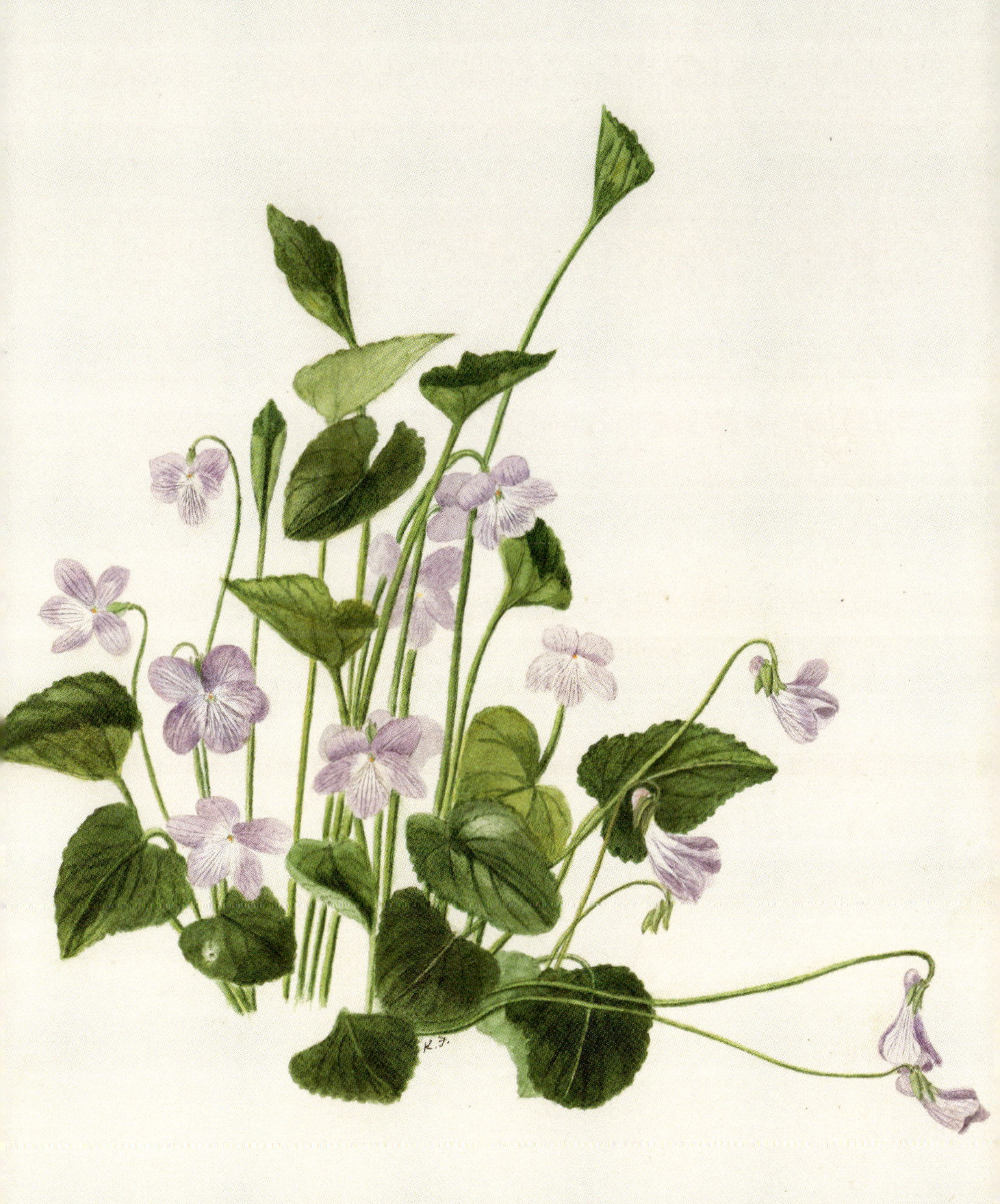

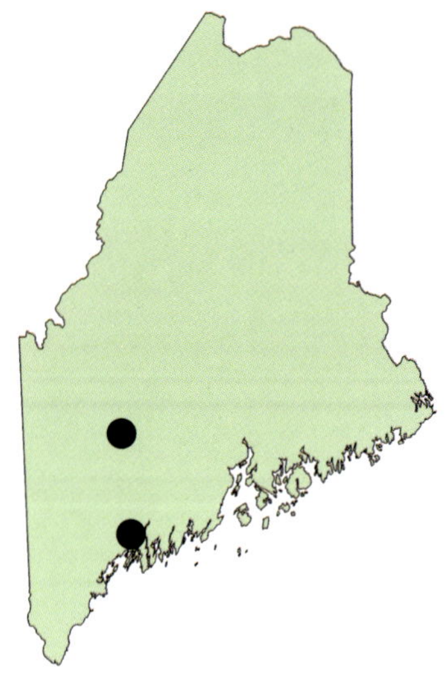

Moist forest, damp meadows, edges of swamps and bogs

Furbish Observed At:

Brunswick (1871)
Chesterville (n.d.)

GREATER PURPLE-FRINGED BOG ORCHID

Platanthera grandiflora

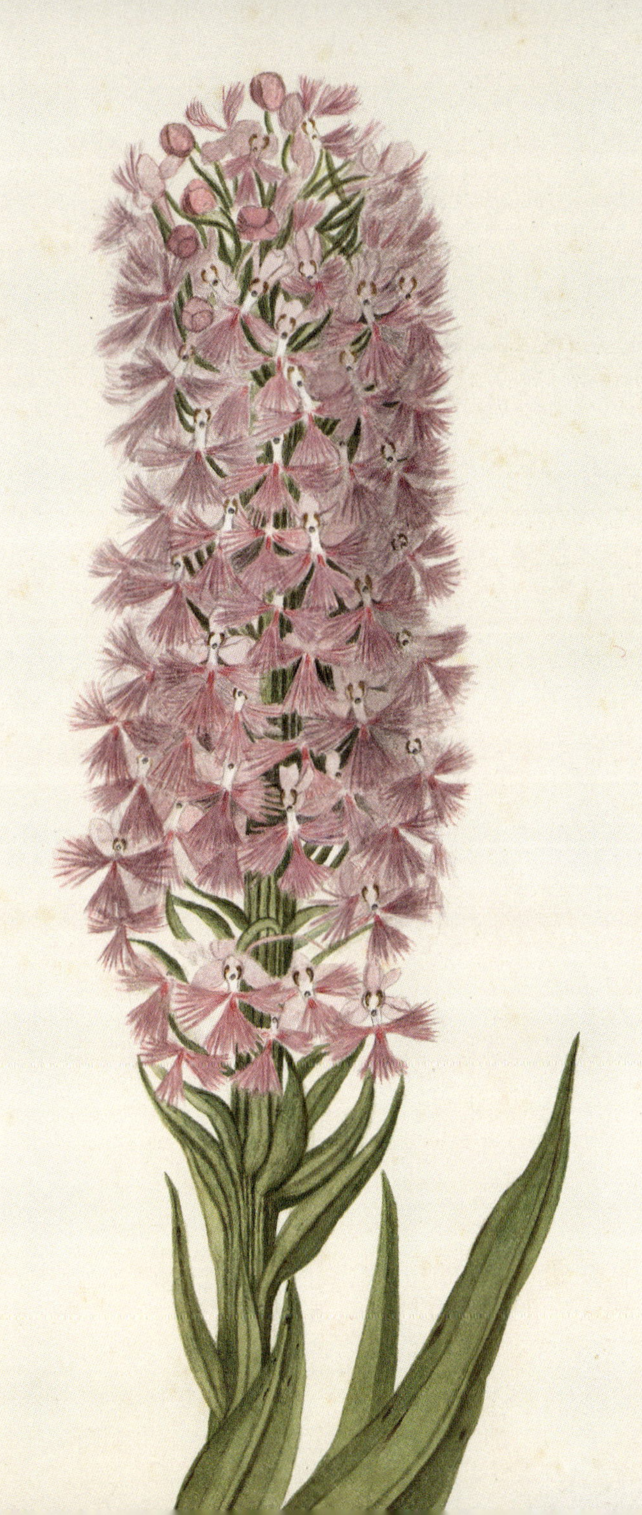

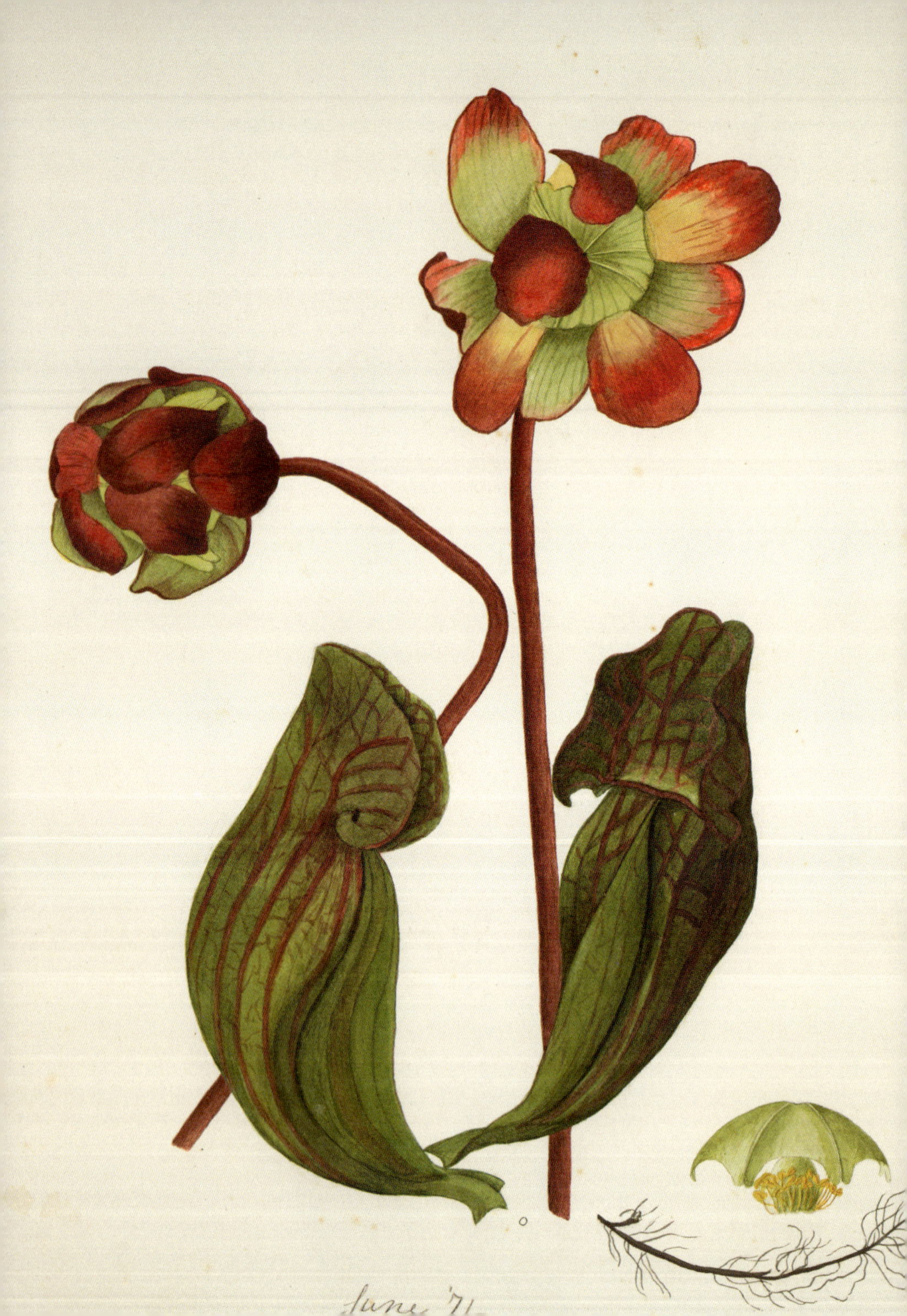
June '71

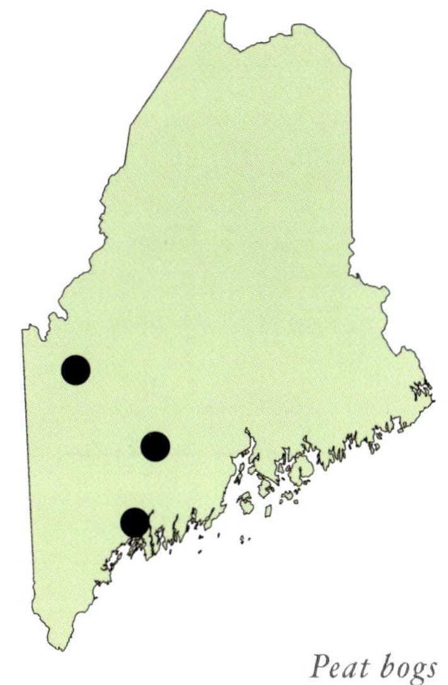

Peat bogs

Furbish Observed At:

Fayette (1871)
Rangeley (1882)
Brunswick (n.d.)

PURPLE PITCHER PLANT

Sarracenia purpurea

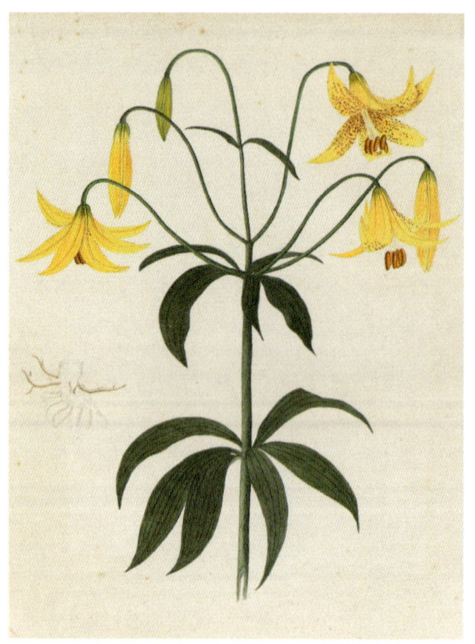
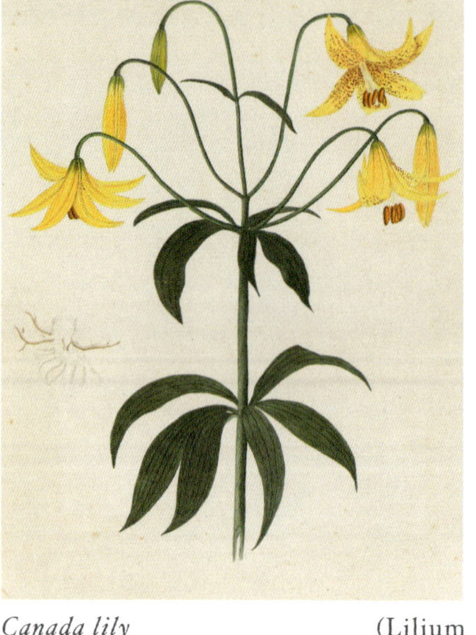

Canada lily (Lilium canadense)

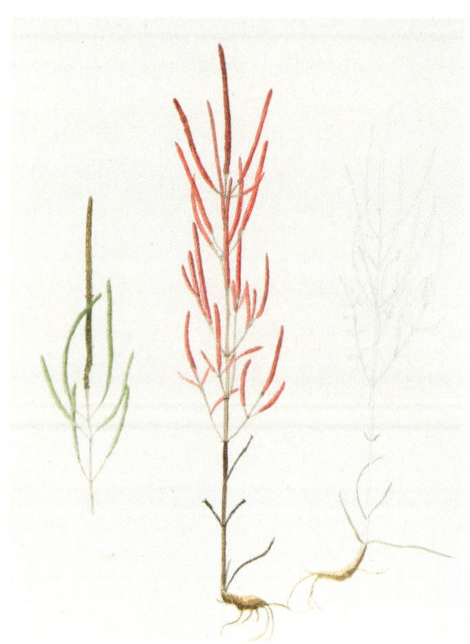

Common glasswort (Salicornia depressa)

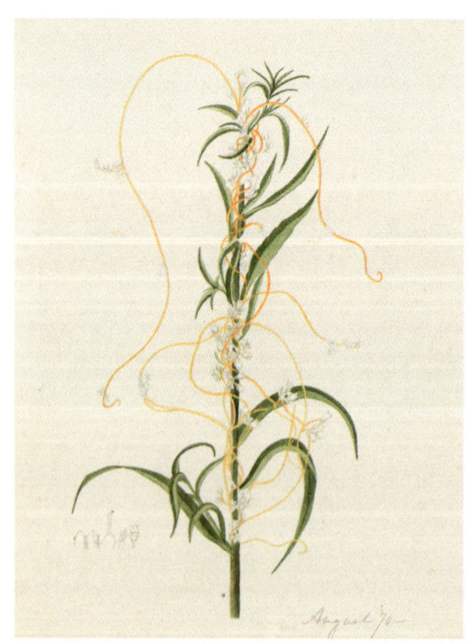

Common dodder (Cuscuta gronovii)

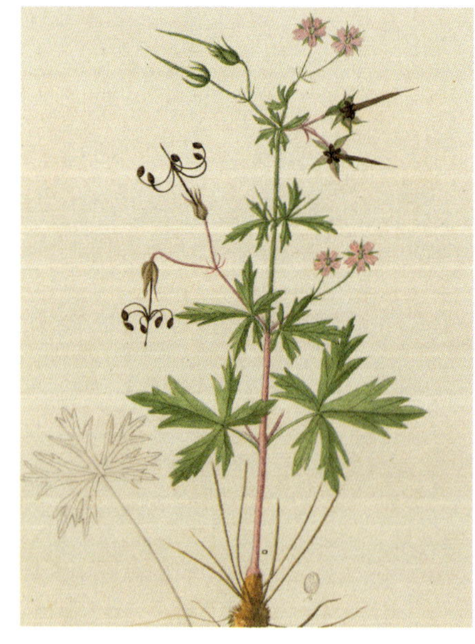

Northern crane's bill (Geranium bicknellii)

All who study or hold dear the plants of Maine owe Kate Furbish a debt of gratitude; as her friend, Merritt Fernald stated, "through her undaunted pluck and faithful brush, [she] has done more than any other to make known the wonderful flora of the 'Garden of Maine.'"

I remember vividly my first acquaintance with Miss Furbish, who when I was a very small boy, visited my home at Orono, spending the summer there making drawings of the native plants. I used to watch her by the hour at her painting, and through the forty odd years succeeding, kept in close with her. . . . I remember visiting her at her home, and her feeling that every minute must be utilized in going over her botanical questions, or in filling in details of her drawings, and that meal-time and sleep-time were absolute nuisances. This intense devotion to the work she had started was one of the most marked characteristics of Miss Furbish, and as you know, when she became enfeebled, she still persisted in working every minute she possibly could.

— Merritt Lyndon Fernald, in a letter to Louise Coburn

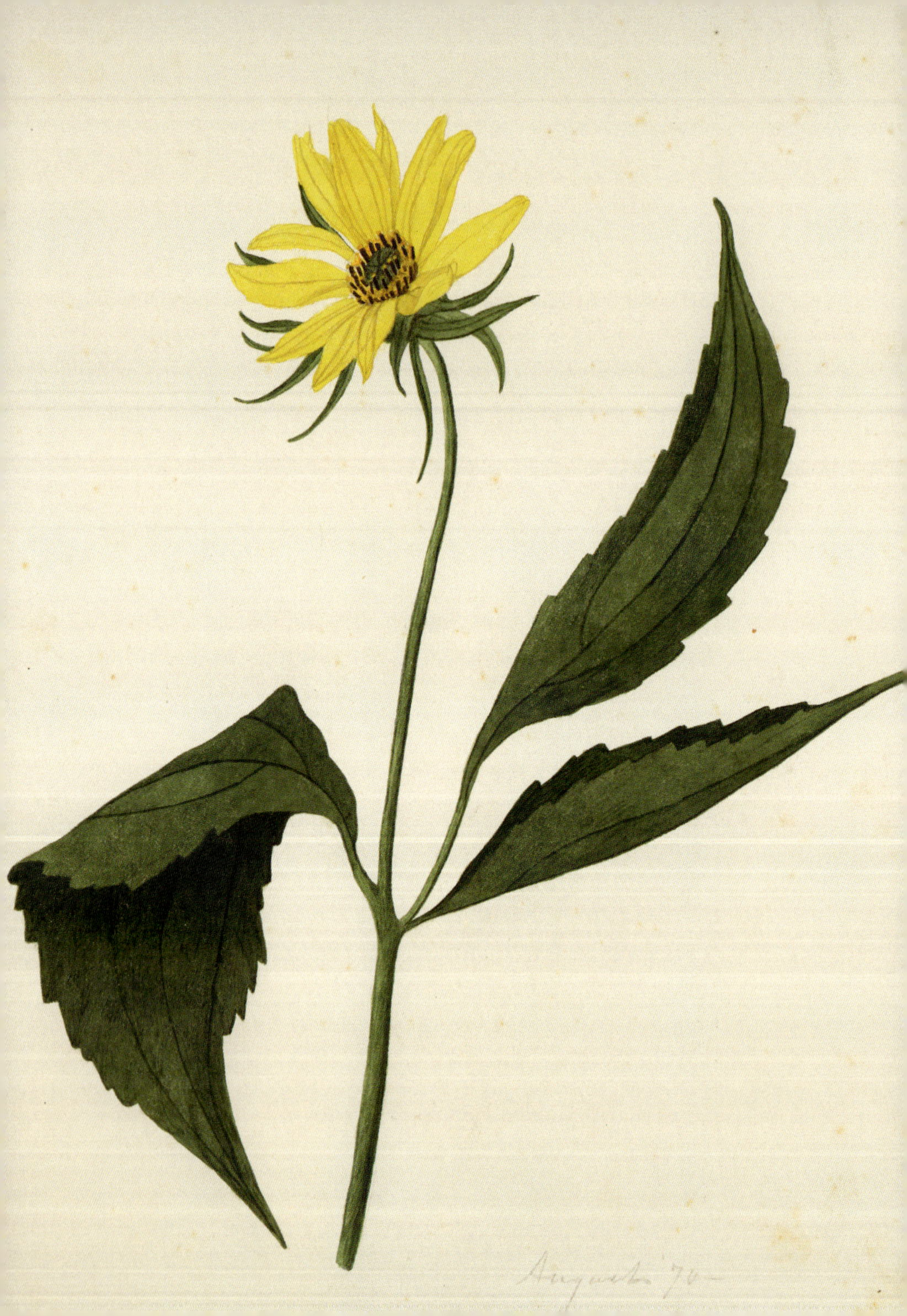
August '70

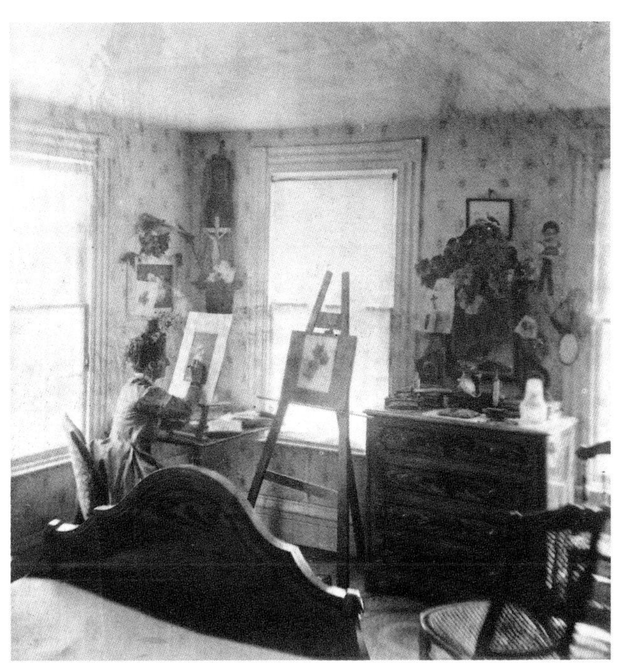

Kate Furbish working in her bedroom studio.

SUNFLOWER EVERLASTING

Heliopsis helianthoides

SOURCES

Bailey L.H. 1923. George Lincoln Goodale. *Rhodora* 25:117-120.

Bonta M.M. 1991. *Women in the field: America's pioneering women naturalists.* College Station (TX): Texas A&M University Press.

Chamberlain E.B. 1909. Bull. Josselyn Bot. Soc. no. 3.

Coburn L.H. 1925. Kate Furbish: botanist: an appreciation. [Place unknown: publisher unknown].

Collins, F.S. 1906. George Edward Davenport. *Rhodora* 10:1-10.

Coxe M. 1842. The claims of the country on American females. Columbus (OH): Isaac N. Whiting.

Davenport G.E. 1899. The ferns of Maranacook, Maine. *Rhodora* 1:218-220.

Davenport G.E. 1906. A hybrid Asplenium new to the flora of Vermont. *Rhodora* 8:12-15.

Day M. 1901. The herbaria of New England. *Rhodora* 3:241.

Fernald M.L. 1895. Supplement to the second edition of the Portland catalog of Maine plants. Proc. Portland Soc. Nat. Hist. 2:129.

Fernald M.L. 1899a. The rattlesnake-plantains of New England. *Rhodora* 1:2-7.

Fernald M.L. 1899b. Two plants of the Crowfoot Family. *Rhodora* 1:48-52.

Fernald M.L. 1926. Kate Furbish, botanist (book notice). *Rhodora* 28:36.

Furbish K. 1873-1908. Maine flora. 16 volumes. Kate Furbish Collection. Located at: George J. Mitchell Department of Special Collections & Archives, Bowdoin College Library, Brunswick, (ME); M70.1.

Furbish K. 1876-1897. Historic letters: Kate Furbish. 33 items. Archives of the Gray Herbarium. Located at: Harvard University Herbaria & Library, Cambridge (MA).

Furbish K. 1881. A botanist's trip to "The Aroostook." *American Naturalist* 15:69-70.

Furbish K. 1882. A botanist's trip to "The Aroostook," no. 2. *American Naturalist* 16:397-399.

Furbish K. 1899. *Myosotis collina* in Maine. *Rhodora* 1:76.

Furbish K. 1901. *Cardamine bellidifolia* in Cumberland County, Maine. *Rhodora* 3:185.

Graham A., Graham F., Jr. 1995a. *Kate Furbish and the Flora of Maine*. Gardiner (ME): Tilbury House.

Graham A., Graham F., Jr. 1995b. Kate Furbish: a founding member. Bull. Josselyn Bot. Soc. no. 12.

Gray A. 1848. *A Manual of the Botany of the Northern United States*. Boston (MA): J. Munroe.

Gray A. 1858. *How Plants Grow: A Simple Introduction to Structural Botany with a Popular Flora.* Toronto: Adam Miller.

Gray A., Robinson B.L., Fernald M.L. 1908. *Gray's New Manual of Botany: A Handbook of the Flowering Plants and Ferns of the Central and Northeastern United States and Adjacent Canada.* 7th ed. New York: American Book Company.

Haines A. 2011. New England Wild Flower Society's *Flora Novae Angliae*. New Haven (CT): Yale University Press.

Marvinney R. 2002. *Simplified Bedrock Geologic Map of Maine.* Augusta (ME): Dept. of Conservation, Maine Geologic Survey; [accessed 2015 February 19]. www.maine.gov/dacf/mgs/pubs/online/bedrock/bedrock11x17.pdf

Pease A.S. 1951. Merritt Lyndon Fernald 1873–1951. *Rhodora* 53:33-65.

Rudolph E.D. 1990. Women who studied plants in the pre-twentieth century United States and Canada. *Taxon* 39 (2):151 205.

Watson S. 1881-1882. Proc. Amer. Acad. Arts 17:375.

Yang, S, Pfister D.H. 2006. *Monotropa uniflora* Plants of Eastern Massachusetts Form Mycorrhizae with a Diversity of Russulacean Fungi. *Mycologia* 98(4): 535-540.

In 1908, self-taught botanist and artist Kate Furbish presented Bowdoin College with a monumental collection of 1,326 approximately life-size renderings of flowering plants and conifers that were growing in Maine at the time. Representing her life's work, the botanical drawings and watercolor paintings are mounted on large paper sheets and gathered in fourteen bound volumes that are nearly two feet tall. Furbish's work has a permanent place in the George J. Mitchell Department of Special Collections & Archives at the Bowdoin College Library.

Grateful acknowledgment is made to the Bowdoin College Library for permission to reproduce in this volume a small sampling of Furbish's illustrations of Maine's flowering plants.